Restaurant Gordon Ramsay

A Story of Excellence

Restaurant Gordon Ramsay

★ ★ ★

By
Gordon Ramsay

Recipes with
Matt Abé

Photography by John Carey

Contents

Introduction: Now and Then

In 2020 I found myself diving in the pristine waters of the Great White Highway of Tasmania for the television series *Uncharted*. These waters are home to an extraordinary range of sea creatures, including, as the name suggests, great white sharks, which are among the largest animals on the planet. They are not to be messed with, but here I was in their territory, 30 feet down amid long thick strands of kelp, risking life and limb in search of huge crayfish and afraid to look over my shoulder; it was like something out of *Finding Nemo*. I wanted to find the crayfish because I'd been told there was nothing quite like them, and then get the hell out of there.

We were using a diving system I'd never used before called snuba, where air is supplied from long hoses connected to compressed air cylinders on the surface. As I battled to keep the hose from strangling me and praying I didn't run into a great white shark, I was also thinking about what my guide had told me just before we plunged into the water. Apparently, six months earlier his best friend had been bitten by a great white while scallop diving.

'Is he ok?' I asked.

'Tragically, not. He was bitten in half by the great white and died. It was truly awful.'

I like to push the limits; I love to explore and know where the very best produce comes from, to live and breathe it, to fear nothing, but his words made me question my sanity. What the hell was I doing in this terrifying place?

Before diving, we'd also talked about how to catch these spiny crayfish. If you want to discover the magic, you've got to crawl into crevices and find them. They're not going to serve themselves up on a plate.

So here we were, both underwater, my guide moving through the kelp with ease. Suddenly, he shimmied towards some rocks, signalling 'Follow me, follow me'. He was only 5ft 7in, much smaller than me, so when he squeezed underneath a rock ledge and pulled his air hose down, bam! He'd gone. I couldn't see him. As I'm 6ft 3in, I found myself thinking there's no way in hell I'm squeezing through the same gap, but knew I had to try. So I pulled my air hose down and made my way into that

crevice. Unfortunately, only the top of my torso would fit inside, so now I was stuck and, worryingly, I'd lost sight of my guide.

One thing I've always believed, whatever situation you find yourself in, is always to look for a solution. Find the best outcome. Life is too short to fret. Keep moving forward. So where, I thought, is my way out? I pushed out of the gap and started to climb back up when I suddenly saw what I most feared – a 3.5 metre great white shark in front of me. It was both mesmerising and horrifying.

We had gone through all the protocol of what to do if we came across one, including lying on the floor and staying still until it moved on. But my instinct was flight, so I dived back down the crevice faster than a rat up a drainpipe and it turned out I *could* fit through the gap; I just needed a bit more incentive.

As I sat in that nook, my heart racing and wondering what to do, I felt a tapping on the back of my head. It was my guide signalling me to move so we could get out of the crevice. I also noticed he was holding the biggest spiny crayfish I'd ever seen – the reason we were in this predicament to begin with.

I tried to tell him with my own sign language that I'm not moving mate; there's a giant shark up there. This piece of news, however, didn't seem to faze him. He handed me the crayfish and signalled to push up to the surface, so I turned, thinking that we were about to become the shark's afternoon tea, but thankfully it had gone.

Back on the boat, my heart was still racing, and as I struggled to catch my breath, I asked, 'Didn't you see the great white shark?'

And he replied, as calmly as you like, 'Yeah, mate. I told you it's the Great White Highway – they're everywhere.'

In my hand, though, was the most magnificent, powerful and extraordinary crayfish I'd ever seen.

We headed for land and lit a fire on the beach, eating sashimi crayfish with soy and wasabi, and cooking the tail in a pot of boiling water. The yield of meat from that giant crayfish was immense, enough for six people.

The flesh was shimmering and translucent, meaty yet sweet, and absolutely delicious. It was clear to me why these crayfish were so prized, but equally clear that you must be mad to catch one.

I tell this story because food always tastes better when you've earned it, and that's what happens in the restaurant kitchen too. If you want to be the best and use the best produce, you have to sacrifice and work for it. The fruits of your labour and commitment will reward you five-fold. That's the heart and soul of what we have done for 25 years at Restaurant Gordon Ramsay. Taking the plunge and being brave enough to put everything on the line, as I did back in 1998 when I opened the restaurant, was terrifying, but I did it anyway. You can't let fear hold you back from aiming for perfection.

Just two days after my confrontation with the great white, I was back in the kitchen at Royal Hospital Road telling chef patron Matt Abé about my adventures in Tasmania and the island's incredible produce. Next moment he was telling me how stunning the latest ducks were and the new dish he'd been working on that included an incredible black garlic purée. We were doing what all chefs love to do – sharing ideas and getting excited about the creative opportunities we'd have with the best produce we could lay our hands on.

I get re-energised by superb produce and the stories behind them. And the more I engage, the more I am reminded why I started Restaurant Gordon Ramsay and why we as a team continue to push fear aside and pursue excellence every day. You don't deliver perfection by holding back. Bringing drive and commitment to work has changed my life and opened up a world of discovery. As a young chef I could only dream of success, but now I'm living the dream.

It's both humbling and fascinating to look back over the last 25 years of Restaurant Gordon Ramsay at Royal Hospital Road. When I took that plunge into the unknown, my metaphorical great white shark was fear of failure, of not achieving my goal, but I didn't let it stop me, no matter what adversities or mud were thrown my way.

Of course, a lot has changed in two and a half decades, and, thanks to television, everything I do now is much more in the public eye. Millions of people in multiple territories have seen an episode of *Kitchen Nightmares* where I've had to deal with a totally unrealistic restaurant owner who is unable to take advice. When I've let rip, which stems from my desire to improve things, it's captured for entertainment and many people think I am blunt and irascible all the time. I'm not, but television makes certain demands: you have finite time,

you have to be entertaining, the programme is edited for effect. The persona people see on TV is not necessarily who I am. I hope at some level viewers get a sense of what I stand for, what drives me and how much I care.

That's also partly the reason for this book, which I've been thinking about for some time. It tells the story of my career, how I learned my craft and eventually carved my own path, opening the restaurant that remains the core of my entire group, at the heart of everything I do. This book celebrates its importance to me and all those who have worked there, and, I hope, gives an idea of its contribution to British gastronomy.

It's great to be successful, but I think it's important to show how I got there – the sacrifices that had to be made, the bumps in the road that felt like mountains to climb, the moments that helped shape my path, the triumph of reaching a lifelong goal, and what I did once I got there.

The book is also a celebration of the teams who, over the years, have helped Restaurant Gordon Ramsay to continually evolve, set the standard and maintain excellence at every turn. It took years for me to work out my approach to food and my style of cooking, and it makes me very happy that the leaders in the restaurant kitchen have added their voices to that development.

First and foremost, we cook with the seasons, so the book is arranged in that way too. Produce is at its best when in season, so it makes sense to use it as close as possible to the time it is picked, caught or harvested. Failing that, we pickle certain ingredients, such as blackberries and mushrooms, so we can use them out of season and still get great flavour. Trying as much as possible to work seasonally is why a meal in spring, for example, will not be the same as in summer or any other season. Spring is all about asparagus, morel mushrooms and wild garlic; summer about berries, stone fruits and tomatoes; autumn about figs, venison and white truffle; winter about pumpkin, Jerusalem artichokes and rhubarb. This differentiation is important because everything starts with produce: it's our job to elevate it with careful preparation and precise cookery focused on maximum flavour, and to deliver it to guests in its most perfect state.

The book opens with canapés and amuse-bouches, perfect little mouthfuls that hint at the pleasures to come. The recipes that follow them were chosen to represent the range of top-notch produce we use in our finely honed dishes, and the key seasonal ingredients among them are served in favourite ways. The result is a snapshot of the year, but also typical of the last 25 years. The recipes are presented just as we cook them in the

restaurant kitchen, so the ingredient lists are long and the methods include some technical equipment. I don't expect home cooks to attempt them, but feel free to try. At the very least you will see how much time, care and dedication go into producing a three-star meal.

For diners, of course, much of what happens in the background doesn't really concern them. What does matter is that from the moment they arrive at the restaurant to the moment they leave they've been immersed in a magical world of fine food.

Interleaved with seasonal information and the recipes are stories of key moments in my career. These describe how I mastered my craft in the UK under fantastic mentors, and first set myself the goal of one day winning three Michelin stars, and how I went on to earn my stripes in France. These experiences together gave me the foundation and framework to create my own unique dining experience at Restaurant Gordon Ramsay, where I nurtured a workplace of collaboration, a top-notch team truly focused on achieving and maintaining three Michelin stars.

There are many restaurant guides, awards and accolades, but among chefs *The Michelin Guide* has always been the ultimate benchmark of recognition. It helps set a standard of expectation for diners as well. One Michelin star is a great achievement, and recognition of a solid, quality establishment. Two Michelin stars are reward for an exceptional, unique experience and an incredible accolade to receive. Three Michelin stars are rarer than hen's teeth, requiring individuality, consistency and utter perfection at every step. They indicate that a restaurant, wherever it may be in the world, has achieved the pinnacle of excellence. Of course, that's not the end of the story. The effort to maintain those stars requires a laser-like focus and extraordinary will. There is no let-up.

Restaurant Gordon Ramsay has now held three Michelin stars for 22 years. It's important to understand, though, that *The Michelin Guide* doesn't make your business a success, the team does, but the stars it awards are the most coveted within the world of hospitality. They are the standard by which we are measured, and are a wonderful accolade, but what drives us every day is the lasting impact we make on our guests.

I remain as hungry for success as I was 25 years ago, and perfection remains a constant goal because I need a certain level of jeopardy to get my cogs turning. That pressure, of course, is strictly confined to the kitchen. I've always thought that Restaurant Gordon Ramsay is a chance for us to relax our guests and deliver a meal of ultimate indulgence that will live forever in their

memory. They step inside and immerse themselves in the experience. Three hours later, they step out again, full of wonder. Those three hours are pure escapism, a taste of the sublime that has taken two and a half decades to perfect. To achieve that takes an incredible, dedicated team, but to maintain that over 25 years is extraordinary. Long may it continue.

Lightness and Evolution

Finding my voice in food came from hard work, years of mastering my craft, grabbing onto opportunity, following my gut instincts and, to put it simply, seeing the light.

I've never wavered from using the very best ingredients, finding the right composition for a dish, and dressing a plate simply but beautifully. I was constantly seeking ways to show dishes in a new light and, importantly, trying to break free from the rich and heavy cookery traditions of Britain's past. It's what has set me apart from my contemporaries.

Finding the DNA of my food – working out what I wanted it to be like and what principles were involved – was a key step because only then would evolution be possible. Great cooking never stands still, it evolves, and evolution is a conscious process requiring measured decisions, and not succumbing to change unless it's necessary and for the better.

I believe it's vital to recognise fads and fashions in food, and to judge whether they are sustainable. It's a mistake to get caught up in the hype, but important to listen, watch and learn while staying true to your vision. Things become popular for a reason, and sometimes there are nuggets of magic in the latest craze, but jumping on every bandwagon will see you on a road to nowhere fast. At the time of writing there's been lots of talk about plant-based eating, factory-made meat substitutes, the genetic modification of foodstuffs … lots of interesting ideas about what's best for the planet. We always try to listen and learn.

At Restaurant Gordon Ramsay, we focus on staying true to our principles, leading the way in showing what's possible on the plate and in the dining room when perfection and superb produce underpin every effort we make. Key staff are given the autonomy to express themselves, but the restaurant holds onto the style I established. The path to that point began in 1987, when I joined the kitchen of Marco Pierre White at Harvey's in south London. There I worked my way up to sous chef, his right-hand man, running the place in his absence so he could go on holiday. To this day I am very grateful for the arse-kicking Marco gave me when I was young, and equally for the confidence he showed in me. He knew I was a vital part of his team, so to stop me from leaving,

he told me that Le Gavroche was full and had no space for me to join its brigade. When I finally did, they asked, 'What took you so long to get here? We could have taken you a year ago!'

It was smart of Marco to hold onto me for as long as possible, and I respect his reasons for doing that. He not only nurtured my competitive spirit, but got me into the kitchens of Le Gavroche in Chelsea. Under Albert and Michel Roux, Le Gavroche was a French powerhouse, determined to put London on the culinary map. At the time, British food had an awful reputation and was very much a poor relation to French cuisine. Through the Roux brothers, France became a gastronomic beacon showing us the way to improve. It was the beginning of the food revolution in the UK, and I knew early on that I needed to immerse myself in the world of French cookery to take British food down a new path. I learned a lot in that great restaurant.

I have to say, though, that a major turning point in my career was getting into the Paris kitchen of Guy Savoy, where I built on the foundations I had established earlier. I was suddenly privy to the light touch of a two-star chef driving for three stars, an experience I'd draw inspiration from down the track with Restaurant Gordon Ramsay. I believe the jump from two to three stars is the most pivotal move. Others claim that going from one to two stars is more important, but I've made that jump several times, so I don't buy that view. At Guy Savoy I witnessed at first hand what the push to three stars really involves, and it had the most profound impact on me.

Meanwhile, though, I had to swallow my pride and take a step back to commis chef to become a better cook. The first three months at Guy Savoy I was relegated to pastry and, even worse, churning sorbet. Ten different flavours, all churned to order and taken upstairs on a trolley to the guest. I could churn in my sleep. And that's the point: the work was boring me. No one knew what I was capable of. It was hard to stomach, but I knew it was the only way forward.

It's well known that it can take 10 years to rise to sous chef, so I had to prove myself – and quickly. The first step was to become fluent in French so I could excel in any given situation in the kitchen. I wanted to understand

every nuance, every technique and explanation so I could store away that knowledge and use it to my benefit. Eventually, I got my chance on the fish section and hit a home run. I was back in my element and ready to excel.

Guy had an incredible lightness in his food, something I'd never experienced before. Everything was delicate and frothy, and he was thickening his sauces with things such as a purée of roasted celeriac. This delivered something beautiful, making dishes lighter without losing the big flavours. It was a revelation, and shifted my thoughts about cooking, planting the seed for my own style in the kitchen.

I was also energised by the amazing things he did with flavours, such as infusing fish stock with Madagascan vanilla pods, then whisking in butter to make it almost mousse-like. It was a fantastically light accompaniment to his sea bass dish and made me see ingredients differently. Another thing that blew my mind was that he served the fish with the scales on, as their oils enhanced the flavour and protected the flesh. In addition, the scales stood up during cooking, so the fish ended up looking like a hedgehog on the plate.

This technique was unheard of in Britain, but Guy was adamant that it helped retain the flavour of the fish, which is what mattered most to him. Of course, if, on my return to the UK, I had dared to serve fish with scales on, critics would have roasted me, and guests would have been perplexed. British food wasn't quite ready for that step, and, to be honest, I've never been convinced that fish should be served like that. When I eventually opened Restaurant Gordon Ramsay, I kept Guy's cooking technique for sea bass, but always peeled the scales off before plating up. As for using vanilla in the dish, people's reaction was perhaps predictable: 'What are you doing messing with dessert ingredients?'

From Guy I also learned to respect produce and use every part of it, a different approach from Marco at Harvey's, where, for example, we tended to use only the white part of a leek, and threw the rest away. At Guy Savoy we used the white part for a dish, and the green parts in sauces, mousses or even staff meals. A nose-to-tail cooking policy applied to every item of produce, not just proteins.

Thanks to Guy I found a new way of thinking about cooking focused on quality produce, big flavours, supreme technique and, most importantly for British cuisine, lightness. I had found the key to freeing British food from its poor reputation and turning it on its head.

Apart from learning this new approach to cookery, I loved the focus on freshness and precision too – ordering in the exact amounts required per day, taking delivery in time for service, and creating the tightest possible link between source and plate. It was the most exciting revelation I'd had in my career. It worked beautifully and I filed it away for future use. It also changed diners' perceptions of modern British food.

I came back to London in 1993 with a head full of steam, convinced that what I'd learned from Guy gave me a uniqueness that no other chef in London had at that time. I cut back on the use of butter and cream, and broke away from overpowering hero ingredients with stodgy sauces. Instead, I served aerated sauces, silky veloutés and fresh purées that connected everything on the plate. These became the hallmarks of my cooking, and are now, I'm pleased to say, a defining feature of fine dining.

My insistence on using the very best produce and maintaining a light touch are intrinsic to the approach at Restaurant Gordon Ramsay. Take scallops, for example. We have always used hand-dived ones from the west coast of Scotland because they are extraordinary, and to this day we prepare them in a time-honoured way. We open them using the sharpest knife possible so the lid comes off cleanly, and then scoop out the flesh, ensuring we take every single bit. After that we cook them very simply, then this is where evolution comes in.

Back when I started the restaurant, I was serving scallops with a cauliflower purée and raisin vinaigrette, or with sweetcorn purée and quail's eggs. These days Matt serves them with caviar sauce, a beurre blanc and a touch of sriracha; or with ajo blanco, verjus, grapes and olive oil; or with violina pumpkin, clementine and shiso; or even as a tartare. At the heart of each variation, though, is still that glorious scallop served with a lightness of touch – we're just dressing it in different clothes. The dish remains true to the principles I established, and that's the important part that has carried through the last 25 years.

The food DNA I have built has given my chefs the foundation to flourish. We create new dishes by evolving the old ones, but always with lightness at the forefront. All those years ago when I brought this new approach to British food, it was regarded as maverick, and I think it took people by surprise. But my way was not just about bringing in lightness – there have been other changes too. Chief among these is presentation, which adds beauty and elegance to every dish. This is part of a new era that I wasn't brought up in, so it owes a lot to the evolution and aspirations of our chefs, who enjoy using their artistic skills to raise dishes to another level. They are now leaders in this wonderful part of the craft.

Through the years, the chef patron (head chef) at the restaurant – whether it's been the current head, Matt Abé, or previous holders Clare Smyth and Mark Askew – has led the team using the underlying principles of my approach to cookery, but also injected their own signature, ethos and culinary nous to an ever-evolving menu. Heading up a Michelin-starred establishment places huge pressure on these incredible chefs. But without exception they have taken the reins of a thoroughbred restaurant, captured the essence of what we do and added parts of themselves too. They have taken it forward and led it into the future.

SACRIFICE

It was 1998. From the outside peering in, my career looked to be accelerating fast in an upward trajectory, but it wasn't going fast enough for me. An urgency to reach the pinnacle, a desire to be the best I could, was eating away at me. I was pushing, but felt I wasn't getting enough traction and that something had to give.

I look back at that rise, and it actually happened much quicker than I felt at the time. I'd spent years earning my stripes with Marco Pierre White at Harvey's and the Roux brothers at Le Gavroche, then honed my skills with Guy Savoy in Paris. Now I desperately wanted an outlet for my ambitions.

I'd first had a taste of empowerment in 1994, when Marco made me head chef of Rossmore in Chelsea, later renamed Aubergine. That restaurant was just a tiny little bistro, but it gave me the chance to prove myself in stages. It was a fascinating five-year project, going from one to two Michelin stars.

The Aubergine team was filled with the most extraordinary and passionate professionals, who got on board with my vision of lightening up modern British cuisine and established an impeccable level of service. Many of the staff became the core of the team at Restaurant Gordon Ramsay. But back then we were just getting started. I had so much more to explore and to give.

Aubergine became the hottest restaurant in town, attracting a starry clientele, and there was a long waiting list to get a table. That period of time was incredible, and imperative for my next step, but I had partners who weren't restaurateurs, so I had mixed feelings about the situation.

Anyone who knows me will tell you I can't sit still. I like to keep moving. Having nailed one goal, I look for the next challenge. So even though Aubergine was a success, I was thinking, 'How can I take my food and restaurant to the next level?' The answer was to go solo and get my own restaurant. I was prepared to fight tooth and nail for it, and one word kept ringing in my head. I grabbed paper and a pen and wrote down the word SACRIFICE in capital letters. Then I underlined it. That word summed up what I needed to do, and it applies to anyone with a burning ambition. You want your dream? Well, you must sacrifice something to get it. You have to work, work, work. You can't get from A to B unless you travel the hard road in between. It's full of bumps, turns and decisions that impact not just on your life, but the lives of those around you too. Sometimes you'll become aware that you haven't made the right decisions, but it doesn't have to be the end of the world. What matters is that you own every decision you make, and find your way through, or you'll never reach your destination.

I'd found my voice on the plate, one that let the seasons direct the path, and developed the restraint required to ensure that everything on the plate served a purpose. Each plate was a perfect representation of a moment in the season, but I knew I had much more in me. I was young and impatient, racing against the clock to get complete control so I could steer things where I wanted.

Tana and I had recently purchased our very first home, a huge moment in our lives. It was a beautiful apartment in Wandsworth, south London, that we bought from fashion designer Jeremy Hackett. It took every penny of our savings, but it was a wonderful reward for the hard work, risks and sacrifices we'd gone through up to that point. It signalled the start of a new phase in our lives, of having greater security and stability.

Then along came Meg, our first child, and I was startled by the responsibility involved in being a parent. It brings a whole different level of pressure – the pressure to give your child the best possible foundation and create opportunities for them. Of course, I adapted to that, and really enjoyed family life. But Aubergine wasn't quite where I wanted it to be because I couldn't run it entirely on my terms. I had partners who didn't understand my objectives. It was time to go out on my own.

The vision for Restaurant Gordon Ramsay was bubbling away in my head. I wanted an agile menu that spoke of the season, dishes that took modern British food into a new era of lightness I'd learned from my time with Guy Savoy. I foresaw a place that would be running on passion, adrenalin and collaborative creativity. A place where, as a diner, you always felt special, and every dish that left the kitchen was magical and perfect. I had in mind dishes that were new, ambitious and not afraid to show a less-is-more approach – dishes such as lobster ravioli, which had a mousse-like filling and was served on a fresh tomato chutney. It was light and adaptable enough to change with the seasons, which is why it's on the menu to this day.

Having decided to strike out on my own, I'd begun negotiations with Pierre Koffmann for his restaurant site on Royal Hospital Road in Chelsea. Pierre was selling up and moving La Tante Claire to The Berkeley Hotel in Knightsbridge. My bid was a long shot and I knew I had little chance of succeeding. No bank would back me because there were only three years left on the lease and I didn't have enough cash. There was only one way I could raise the capital, so I sat down with Tana one night.

'We are going to have to sell our home,' I said.

She looked at me quizzically and asked, 'Why?'

'Because we need the money for a deposit on the lease of the Royal Hospital Road site.'

'What happens if it doesn't work?' she asked.

'Trust me, it's going to work,' I replied. 'You've just got to bear with me.'

She took a moment to consider what I was suggesting.

'For how long?' she asked.

'Five years.'

'So that means Meg will be going to school, I'll be continuing to work as a teacher and we won't have a roof over our heads?'

'Well, we'll have a roof over the restaurant,' I offered.

'You can't sleep in a restaurant!' she said.

So, as we have always done, we talked it through and somehow I convinced her to sell the flat. I was asking a lot of Tana, but her faith in me has always been extraordinary.

It has been well documented that I grew up in what many would consider to be a dysfunctional family – penniless, clothed in hand-me-downs and cast-offs, in a home barely held together by my inspiring mum, who had an incredible knack of feeding us on the thinnest of budgets and bringing colour into our often drab lives. She fought really hard to give us the best chance of a better life, and I put my drive and determination down to her influence. I never wanted to let her down, and that feeling extended to Tana and our child. I knew the importance of family.

It would take me years to get ahead, but my upbringing gave me a valuable quality. I knew how to be poor. I knew how to get by and push on with little or nothing. I knew how to let something go in order to move forward. Of course, that is much easier when you're single and accountable only to yourself. Fortunately, I had Tana behind me all the way. She saw the path ahead, the vision that could help give our kids a good life, and she believed, more than anyone, in my, unswerving will to succeed. Meanwhile, she'd have to do the heavy lifting at home, but she knew we had the skills to manage this sacrifice, and if we did it properly, it would pay off.

Sell the apartment? No problem. Give up the car and walk to work? Easy as pie.

Selling our home gave us a quarter of a million pounds in equity to help convince the bank to lend me a million pounds for the lease on Royal Hospital Road. It was a huge sacrifice because we had to give up everything we'd spent the last 10 years working for. At the time it made sense to me, but it's amazing to think we sacrificed our first home for my first restaurant. One step back to go two steps forward. But little did I know we weren't there yet.

The clanger came when the bank asked, 'So you're running seven days a week. What's the turnover? What's the profit?'

'No,' I said, 'this is a personal thing. We're closing Saturday and Sunday.'

At this, their jaws dropped: 'What do you mean closing Saturdays and Sundays? Aren't they your busiest days?'

'No, Monday is going to be the busiest night. And Tuesday, Wednesday, Thursday and Friday.'

'But you're missing the two most important days.'

I told them that every single day was important, but so was the need to rest. The logic was simple: open Monday to Friday, prep and plan on Saturday, spend Sunday with our families. It was somewhat arrogant of me at the time, but I knew my vision would work. I knew the value of rest, the importance of family, and the drive and energy both give you when you are working 18-hour days as we did back then.

That commitment wasn't enough for the bank. Even with the money from our flat, we could only secure half the loan needed, so I had to find more cash to do the deal. When I told Pierre Koffmann, he said,

'How about you pay me some now, and the rest in a year's time after the success of the first year's trading?'

His offer was generous beyond belief – the final piece of the jigsaw.

Royal Hospital Road was mine.

Canapés and Amuse-bouches

It isn't only what's printed on the menu that makes eating at Restaurant Gordon Ramsay so memorable; it is also the little 'unexpected' elements that come at the beginning and the end of the meal that raise it from a really good dinner to an unforgettable experience. The very first taste is always a small but exquisite canapé to accompany the opening round of drinks. Eaten by hand, these bite-sized morsels have to punch above their weight in order to set the scene for what's to come in just one mouthful. Consequently, they are often striking to look at with interesting or contrasting textures and bold flavours. A good canapé should always leave you wanting more.

After the canapé, but before the first course, the chefs have an opportunity to show the diners a little of what they can expect by serving an amuse-bouche, or pre-starter, of their choosing. Like everything else on the menu, it is heavily influenced by the seasons, but because it doesn't have to be planned in advance, it can change daily, depending on what enticing ingredients we have to play with on the day. We have regular favourites that appear annually, but this is a much-enjoyed opportunity to be spontaneous, creative and playful. Like the canapés, these are small dishes designed to entice the palate rather than spoil the appetite.

Selection of Canapés (overleaf)

Cured Fish
Cured Kingfish, Toasted Nori, Dashi Vinegar, Truffle
Cured Sea-Trout, Summer Herbs, Calamansi

Gougères
Smoked Montgomery Cheddar and Pickled Walnut
Comté and Black Truffle

Tartlets
Rove de Garrigues, Spring Flowers
Barbecued Pumpkin, Marinated Trout Roe
Young Peas, Ham, Mint
Cured King Fish, Sesame, Nori
Whipped Lardo, Iberico Ham, Allium

Chips 'n' Dip

With its combination of strong flavours and contrasting textures, this canapé
– an intense French onion dip covered with half caviar and half French onion
consommé jelly, and served with delicate, crisp potato tuiles – makes a real
impact at the very beginning of the meal.

Porthilly Oysters, Elderflower Mignonette

The freshest oysters from the Cornish coastal village of Porthilly are served with a twist on the classic mignonette shallot dressing; we use our homemade elderflower vinegar to bring a fragrant sweetness to the oysters, then garnish them with pretty pink and white elderflowers.

Young Peas, Dashi Custard, Caviar, Hazelnuts

In this celebration of the arrival of spring, we combine peas, the caviar of the land, with true caviar from the sea. The overtones of hazelnut present in the caviar are reinforced by folding a little hazelnut oil through the peas, then both are arranged on top of a savoury dashi custard and garnished with young pea shoots and white garlic and yellow brassica buds.

Tomato Dashi

Tomatoes are at their ripest during the summer, and we treat them with due reverence by distilling their flavour into this incredibly clear consommé that is both clarified and enriched by adding kombu, an edible kelp used to make the Japanese broth called dashi. Served with a profusion of summer herbs, this is a refreshing and fragrant hit of umami.

Bacon and Eggs

Our interpretation of a British classic: a delicate but punchy bacon mousse
hides beneath silky, slow-cooked egg yolk, which is garnished with crispy shallot
crumb and chopped chives. It is served with a handmade grissini wrapped in
finely sliced cured pig's cheek, which acts as a 'soldier' for dipping into the egg.

Beef Consommé, Shallot and Thyme Parker House Roll

A shot of warming beef consommé sets the scene for our diners in winter, providing a rich, luxurious and incredibly flavourful start to the meal. A light and buttery Parker House roll flavoured with shallot and thyme is served on the side to balance the intensity of the beautiful clear soup.

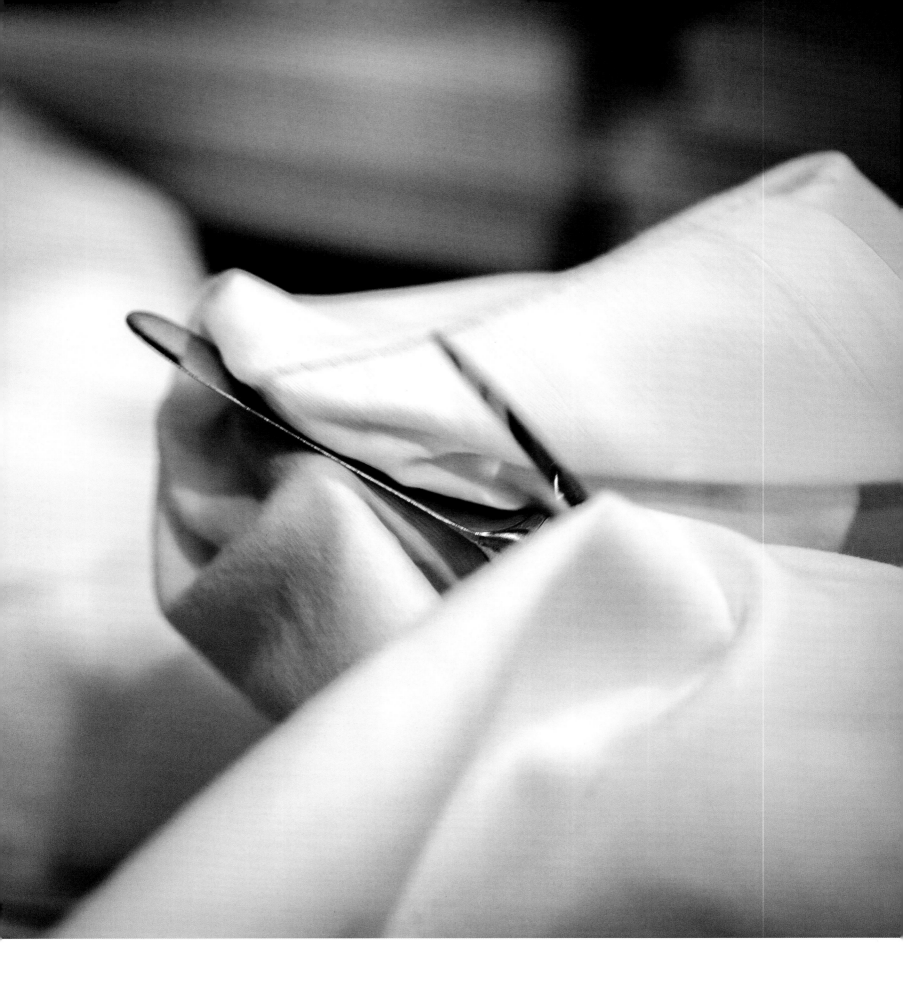

HUNGER PANGS

Once I secured the lease on the Royal Hospital Road site, I got busy planning the business. Restaurants aren't just about food; everything, from organising the kitchen and dining room to greeting and serving the guests, must undergo the most precise attention to detail.

I gave myself four weeks to gut and remodel the premises before reopening as Restaurant Gordon Ramsay. The design of what had been La Tante Claire reflected Pierre Koffmann's vision, so I decided sadly that it all had to go. I had a limited budget, so I got the help of a small interior design firm I'd used on an earlier project. The entire front of house space was gutted, leaving a concrete shell that resembled a bombsite. Given the tight schedule, it was decided to keep the design simple, and use things that were easy to fabricate and install.

The main risk we took was paying £10,000 to an artist called Barnaby Gorton to paint a dreamy blue and grey mural. Fortunately, he quickly grasped the brief and the tight deadline, and his artwork really brought the room to life. We were delighted, and went on to use him on many other projects.

It was a stomach-churning race to get the restaurant finished on time. In fact, the front desk was still being assembled just half an hour before we opened. However, I was happy with what had been achieved. Once there was enough money in the bank, I planned to take the design and fit-out to the next level.

While the place was being renovated, I was writing menus, refining and finalising dishes, and working on a new charter for the way the kitchen and front of house team would run. The deadline was incredibly optimistic, but I had the advantage of bringing with me most of the team from Aubergine, who all saw my vision and wanted to be part of what I wanted to build. With no new staff to train, the focus was on sharpening minds and pre-existing skills to deliver the individual style required to achieve three Michelin stars.

I found being free of the corporate set-up that governed Aubergine really liberating. No longer were there multiple other opinions demanding to be heard, opinions that made me feel constrained and underachieving. I now had the freedom to move on and aim higher. My opening night menu would show I meant business. Glorious seafood and fish, such as lobster and sea bass, would take centre stage, and these would be underpinned by fantastic fruit and vegetables, including summer berries and stone fruits, fennel, peas, courgettes and artichokes. With tomatoes at their best too, I also decided to take my signature lobster ravioli to the next level by presenting it on a fresh tomato chutney. While the dish can work with various ingredients in different seasons, tomatoes make the perfect foundation for it in summer, and the combination would showcase the finesse and lightness I'd been developing ever since I worked with Guy Savoy in Paris.

Of course, I was nervous as hell about what was at stake, so imagine how I felt on the night we opened when ITV ran a show called *Britain's Most Unbearable Bosses*, for which they'd secretly filmed me dressing down a member of staff. It was just a bit of hot air, but the timing – even though the programme went out quite late – couldn't have been worse. We were about to have a full restaurant of paying guests expecting to have the night of their lives while I was being shown having a rant. Refusing to let it distract me, I put my head down, stayed in the kitchen and focused on what mattered.

By 5pm the dining room looked immaculate – 14 tables set for 45 guests. We were all full of nervous energy. First impressions, particularly in the context of a restaurant, are vital, and with the British media standing in judgement, it wasn't hard for emotions to boil over. Any heated words in the run-up were just a symptom of the pressure to achieve perfection.

At 7pm our first-ever guests arrived and the kitchen got into full swing, but before long the extraction fans packed in because the fan belt snapped. It was 59°C in there, hotter than the Sahara. We needed an electrician, but couldn't get one to come until the following morning. Then, just to make things a little more challenging, the air-conditioning went down in the dining room too. Exactly what you need when you're charging guests £100 a head. It was literally the hottest restaurant in town, but the guests didn't seem to mind.

That opening night was a baptism of fire, but the next day we discovered we were fully booked for three months ahead. This was great news, as it meant we were positive in cash flow. That would be music to the bank's ears and mean I could honour the financial arrangement I'd made with Pierre Koffmann.

My idea of the perfect restaurant was crystal clear in my mind, but it would have been pointless if the business were not viable, so getting off to a good start was a huge boost. Financial awareness is hugely important, but when young chefs talk to me about a dish they've created – I love hearing their passion and enthusiasm – very few ever consider if it works commercially. Will they sell those ingredients for five times more than they bought them? In that respect, it doesn't matter what you want to build; you must make the numbers work. That gives you the foundation to create the magic.

The pressures during the early days of the restaurant were insane, but I've always had an element of fearlessness tempered with realism when it comes to opportunity. I liken it to standing on a 10 metre diving board. Many people spend too long looking down, gazing at the bottom of the pool rather than the water level, so they see the distance they have to go as much further away than it actually is. The same is true with a business: the point at which you break through is closer than you think. You have to focus on diving (or cooking) properly to get where you want to be.

It's a very odd experience because you need to be both selfish *and* selfless. You cannot make a successful restaurant without sharing your vision with a select few who can help create that vision. Who those people are becomes obvious the moment you work with them. Successful restaurants are one team, one dream, and if you don't have that, you're out of business. Among my trusted few were Marcus Wareing, Angela Hartnett, Mark Askew and Mark Sargeant. I couldn't have done it without them.

When you open a restaurant and you're pushing to be the best, you get tunnel vision and want no distractions. For me, the distraction was outside negativity: 'Is he going to burn out?' 'Is he ever going to achieve his goal?' People assumed I wanted to be number one, but that was never my aim. I wanted my restaurant to be in the top five because I knew the people in front of me had been there for a long time and had earned their place, just as I was trying to earn mine.

Of course, I wanted three Michelin stars, and I put myself under relentless pressure along the way to that goal. Some days I would crash and burn; other days I found an extra gear. Being fully booked kept me going because I knew the business could prosper. After that, the most important thing became focusing on excellence and achieving consistency.

You only need to watch the documentary series *Boiling Point*, which followed me 24/7 over a period of eight months, to see what impact the pressure was having on me. The filming was at times very intrusive, capturing the birth of our twins for instance. Some days I would stagger home to bed and wake up with a microphone on. To have allowed this degree of access might seem a bit stupid, but I wanted to give a real insight to my life at the sharp end of fine dining. I wanted people to know the extreme determination I had and the level of perfection I was striving for.

As a youngster, being a chef never crossed my mind. My ambition was to become a professional footballer. I spent years learning the skills and playing my heart out, only for injury to ruin my dream. In an odd way, though, football led me to perhaps the ultimate team sport – restaurants. All the determination, ambition and take-no-prisoners mentality that I brought to the game manifested in my cooking career. This time I'd allow nothing to stop me.

I'd seen many talented chefs fail because they didn't understand how to run a business. That, I vowed, would not happen to me. So I secretly studied various failing restaurants behind the scenes. What was going wrong? Why were they running out of steam? How could I avoid repeating their mistakes? My observations made me streamline my own business by setting strict food costings and ruthless margins on wine, by calculating labour costs as a percentage of turnover, and by not taking a proper wage for the first few years. These steps would help to breathe air into the lungs of the business while I focused on producing food of utter perfection in my particular style. There would be no distractions.

I wanted everything to move quickly, but rushing is not compatible with creating three-star food on a plate. It needs time and technique, and I had to push the brigade not just to keep up high standards, but to raise them. I also had to trust my hand-picked front-of-house team to deliver a very special experience. It worked, because we were awarded two Michelin stars after just one year. That was wonderful, but I already knew what that felt like at Aubergine. My goal was three stars, an accolade I was desperate to win.

Unfortunately, I messed up. I got wind that Michelin inspectors would be coming in to review the restaurant, and I stupidly told the TV crew that was still with us. They filmed the arrival of the inspectors from a car across the road from the restaurant, and the microphone I was wearing captured my reaction. I lost out because of that.

The inspectors said the cooking was exemplary and the service faultless, but they also said I should not have told the world they were in for dinner. Without that blunder, I could have won three Michelin stars a year earlier than I did. My excitement ran away with me. I was 31 and racing to be the youngest three-star chef in Britain. I had blinkers on and lost that acute peripheral vision you need when running restaurants.

That moment was hard, but I look back and see it as the result of extreme pressure. The TV series captured this, along with the good and the bad, the exciting and the dreadful. It showed everything the public never normally sees – the distilled determination that can boil over behind the scenes. Viewers' reactions were mixed: some disliked what they saw, others were more sympathetic. All I hoped was that they had gained a better understanding of what is involved in achieving three Michelin stars.

What I do know is that the £200,000 fee I was paid for letting in the cameras helped me to build the restaurant. It allowed me to hire three more staff front of house and three more people in the kitchen, as well to get beautiful chairs for the dining room. Yes, the series may not have shown me in the best light, but I refuse to be embarrassed about that time. I learned from it and, despite what some might think, definitely have more control than I did back then.

The verdict from Michelin was a huge blow but it sharpened my resolve. I was never going to stop until that third star had arrived.

I'll tell you what, though ... it was a really long 365 days until the release of the next Michelin guide.

Spring

There's always something particularly invigorating and exciting about spring. The days get warmer, and everything switches from shades of brown to vibrant colours again. Along with that, extra hours of sunlight bring a new cycle of young produce and, importantly, new opportunities on the plate. All of a sudden, the kitchen brigade is brimming with renewed enthusiasm in just the same way that diners thrill to the idea of eating at one of the world's very best restaurants. Their anticipation is intense and may be fired, for instance, by the season's first asparagus coming through the kitchen door. It provokes a sense of celebration, and is one of the joys of being a chef.

To create a perfect dish, it's vital to start with perfect produce. And capturing produce at just the right moment is a matter of careful timing, which is why we work closely with our farmers and suppliers. These peak moments inspire our chefs to focus on excellence, require supreme attention to detail and allow the team to elevate spring's bounty of young produce to an exceptional eating experience.

In springtime, the magic on the plate is pared back; there is no need for layers of flavour. Restraint, which has always been part of the DNA in our kitchen, is paramount. However, simplicity on the plate is one of the hardest things to get right. Our way is to allow the natural flavours that harmonise and work together to speak for themselves. The result may appear effortless, but a lot of technique underlies each element of a dish.

The abundance of delicate spring produce – asparagus, morels, peas, Jersey Royal potatoes, carrots and wild garlic – and of pigeon, guinea fowl, and amazing beef and lamb, provides uplifting opportunities for our chefs. The result is a menu that is much lighter than winter's, and more vibrant on the plate. This works perfectly because our guests are looking to eat a little lighter and to explore new seasonal produce too.

These wonderful ingredients spark creativity in the kitchen and delight in the restaurant. Among our springtime offerings are a gloriously roasted crown of pigeon with pickled girolles, baby fennel and almond cream; a silky, slow-cooked hen's egg with celeriac purée, Iberico ham crumb and roasted hazelnuts; stunning Isle of Skye scallops with macadamia ajo blanco, grapes and a miso glaze; sea-trout escabeche with carrots tossed in Sauternes and saffron dressing; and a light millefeuille with new-season strawberries, elderflower and vanilla.

Inspirational ingredients

Although there are many ingredients the kitchen relies on, there are some that are central to what we do in the restaurant during spring.

Asparagus
We get our first deliveries of asparagus at the very start of the season. Our favourite variety is grown in Provence, southern France, by chef-turned-farmer Jérôme Galis. His asparagus has a beautiful green grass note and a natural underlying nuttiness. It is incredible.

Unlike supermarket asparagus, which is often green from tip to base, Jérôme's includes the white part that has grown under the soil. It adds an extra 5cm to the length of the spears, which can be nearly 30cm long. However, asparagus is graded by diameter rather than length, and we use a large grade called 26 plus. It is extremely thick, with a circumference similar to the neck of a wine bottle. We use every bit of each spear, treating the various parts differently to get the best out of it, as we do with any vegetable.

Asparagus naturally grows towards sunlight, which creates the long straight spears, but we must store them carefully to retain that shape, as their attraction to light continues even after they have been picked. The light in our walk-in fridge is always on, so if we simply put the asparagus in there and left it for a few days, it would naturally start to bend and curl towards the light. For this reason, we place it in a container in complete darkness as we want to maintain those stunning, straight spears.

We prep down the spear, taking the top for our presentation. The middle is used to make a purée, then we chop up the white part at the bottom for an asparagus stock. The spears are cooked in that stock, then the juices left in the pan are turned into the sauce that goes on the dish. Absolutely nothing goes to waste. This is proper nose-to-tail asparagus eating.

In a restaurant there are many elements of dishes that are pre-cooked or par-cooked in advance, but asparagus must be cooked *à la minute*. When we are in service, we take off the tip, wash and trim it, then cook it to order, ensuring it is neither too crunchy nor too soft. We test for this by pushing a little spike gently into the thickest part; when it's tender, it's ready. It's a demanding process and keeps the chefs on their mettle.

The cooking time is a matter of intuition. We place a pan on the stove, add a splash of olive oil and in go the asparagus spears with a pinch of salt. We cover them with a lid and gently agitate the pan to roll the asparagus and seal it before adding a splash of asparagus stock. We then place the lid back on, and the spears both rapidly boil and steam at the same time. In other words, we're cooking on the vapour, and adding another ladleful of stock as required when the previous splash evaporates.

If you're eager to try this lovely ingredient, one of the greatest eating experiences in springtime is our new-season asparagus with smoked egg yolk, morels and wild garlic. Absolutely gorgeous and spring on a plate.

Wild garlic
During the spring, clumps of wild garlic can be found pretty much everywhere in the UK, even in unlikely places, such as Battersea Park in London. It's hugely important in our kitchen, one of the most glorious foraged ingredients we use in the restaurant.

Wild garlic has long, curved leaves and three-sided stems that bear white flowers. When young, the leaves are small and have a delicate flavour of garlic, chive and spring onion, which means they can be eaten raw. Of course, as the plant grows, the leaves develop a stronger flavour, giving a more intense raw garlic experience. At this point it is much better to blanch or sweat them to provide the backbone flavour of a dish. As for the flowers, they make a pretty garnish that lifts many a dish and makes it appear truly spring-like.

The wild garlic we get at the restaurant has been foraged the day before, and we store it with minimal handling, keeping it dry inside an airtight container. We don't allow the fridge temperature to alter it too much, and it's not washed until just before use because moisture will start the wilting process. To ensure it's in optimum condition, we use it within two days of delivery.

In the kitchen we make a purée from the leaves, which becomes part of the foundation of a dish, or we sweat them off and drape them over a dish, in much the same way as wilted spinach leaves. We also make a wild garlic oil that can be used throughout the year. This is perfect for emulsifying with the juices in our spring asparagus dish to form a delicious accompanying sauce.

Young shoots, being so mild, are used raw on a dish, glazed simply with a little olive oil and a sprinkling of salt. When the shoots are larger and thicker, we like to pickle or ferment them for use at another time of the year.

We also enjoy making wild garlic capers from the seed pods left on the plant once the petals have dropped. They look like tiny bunches of grapes, and the kitchen brigade goes out as a group to forage them. Once back at the restaurant, the pods are separated from the clusters, salted for three weeks, then washed and put into jars topped up with champagne vinegar. After that, they are set aside for at least a week, but the longer the better. We can then use them throughout the year and to nuance to just about any dish. They impart a subtle hint of garlic and a burst of acidity that go wonderfully with, for example, beef in late summer or autumn, or chicken in spring.

Morels
Morels are amazing mushrooms with unique qualities. Those we use at the beginning of the season come from Turkey and are delightfully small. Unlike other mushrooms, they are grown in sandy soil, so they have a damp, earthy aroma rather than smelling of woodland.

Although wetting mushrooms is generally a no-no, morels are quite strong and not only withstand a good wash, but demand it to remove the sandy soil clinging to their honeycomb-like structure. We wash them in lukewarm water a minimum of six times to open up that structure and get all the sand out. Once there is no sand or grit at the bottom of the bowl, we drain them on a towel before they are dried on a rack. It's important to wash only what we need for that day, so this process is repeated on a daily basis. It's a labour of love, but morels are truly worth it.

Once the morels are clean, we trim off the foot and dry it to use as a powder, or to make a mushroom stock. Then we focus on the body of the mushroom.

Raw morels are moderately poisonous if eaten in volume, so it's important to cook them. Our preferred method is braising. We start with a little confit shallot, which is essentially brunoise of shallots sweated in a spot of oil until tender and sweet. We then add the morels, a little vin jaune (yellow wine from the Jura) and a pinch of salt, pop a lid on and let things steam. After that we add a touch of mushroom stock and allow the morels to tick over in their own juices. Once they are braised, we take the lid off, add a compound parsley butter and create an emulsion. A splash more vin jaune

is added at the end for a hint of acidity. All these lovely flavours cling to the spaces within the honeycomb structure, which is what makes morels so special.

When we get large morels, we make a farce – anything from a chicken mousse to wild garlic purée, or some smoked duck trimmings and herbs – and stuff them to become the feature of a dish. We start by blanching them gently to make them more malleable, as this allows us to pipe in more of the farce. Once filled, they are wrapped and we poach them again. To finish, we braise them in the same way as small morels. The end result is soft, tender and meaty, with a wonderfully earthy flavour. Bite into them and all the cooking juices explode in your mouth. In fact, it's extraordinary how much juice they hold and how well they carry whatever flavours have been added.

Few ingredients create as much anticipation as morels in spring. They are amazingly versatile, just as able to work with the grassy notes of asparagus and wild garlic as they are with sweet Cornish cod and Jersey Royal potatoes. In spring our kitchen is never without them.

Jersey Royals
It is no exaggeration to say that Jersey Royals are the most beautiful potatoes. Thanks to being grown in seaweed-fertilised soil on the island of Jersey, they have a unique and extraordinary flavour, which the EU has recognised by awarding them a Protected Designation of Origin (PDO). This means that only Royal potatoes grown on Jersey can be called Jersey Royals.

One of the key characteristics of these potatoes is their tissue-thin skin, so delicate that it often breaks or peels back in transit. Inside, though, the texture is firm, dense and not too waxy. This is no ordinary potato, so how best to feature it? Traditional restaurant thinking has long been that a dish requires a big piece of fish or meat as the hero, and that the rest of the dish is merely complementary. Fortunately, this has changed. When our kitchen focuses on spring, the chefs are thinking more about vegetables than proteins.

Jersey Royals are seasonal potatoes, so there is great excitement when they arrive. Such is their creaminess, underpinned by earthiness and saltiness, that they can be the star of a plate, not merely an accompaniment, perfect though they are in that role too. They come in four different sizes, which in ascending order are: Jersey pearls, which resemble small marbles, Jersey mids, Jersey wares, and Jerseys. Regardless of size, though, they are all young, new-season potatoes.

We wash and grade the potatoes when they arrive because we want to ensure consistency in cooking.

Jersey pearls tend to be cooked whole and served as part of a garnish for a dish. Other sizes may be gently cooked in smoked butter and salt before being vacuum-packed and poached in a water bath (this process allows a consistent result).

Given their superb flavour, Jersey Royals can enhance almost any dish. We like to serve the smoked potatoes with Cornish cod, which we confit in beurre noisette and serve with a potato and salted kombu crumb, sautéd morels, and a light herb purée. It's spectacular!

Jérôme Galis Asparagus, Morels, Smoked Egg Yolk, Wild Garlic

To celebrate the arrival of asparagus, we prepare the spears in three different ways – the tips are sautéd, then steamed in a little stock, the stems are puréed to create a vibrant statement on the plate as well as on the palate, and very fine raw slices are added to the garnish for textural contrast and that just-picked fresh flavour. The asparagus is then served with two other key seasonal ingredients, morel mushrooms and foraged wild garlic, for a dish that captures the very essence of spring.

Serves 8

Asparagus Spears

24 large asparagus spears
Olive oil
200ml Asparagus Stock (see below)
Fine sea salt

Trim the asparagus spears to 12cm long, reserving the woody offcuts to be used for the stock. Place a large sauté pan over a medium–high heat; when the pan is warm, add a drizzle of oil, then add the asparagus spears with a pinch of salt. Cover with a lid and sauté for 20 seconds. Add a splash of asparagus stock and cover again with a lid. Keep adding stock, a splash at a time, for 5–8 minutes, until the asparagus is cooked. When cooked, emulsify the stock with a little olive oil, making sure the asparagus is well glazed. Remove from the pan and reserve the juices to make the wild garlic sauce (opposite).

Asparagus Stock

20ml olive oil
Asparagus trimmings, finely sliced
750ml Chicken Stock (see page 289)

Place a heavy-based saucepan over a high heat and add the olive oil. When hot, sauté the asparagus offcuts for 1 minute. Cover with the chicken stock, bring to a simmer and cook for 10 minutes without reducing. Using a hand-held blender, blitz the stock and pass it through a fine-meshed sieve. Cool in a bowl placed over an ice bath, then store in the fridge until needed.

Asparagus Purée

500g asparagus spears
20ml olive oil
150ml Chicken Stock (see page 289)
100g baby spinach leaves
5g Ultratex

Finely slice the asparagus, reserving the sliced woody trimmings separately. Place a heavy-based saucepan over a medium–high heat and pour in the olive oil. Add the asparagus trimmings, season with salt, then sauté for 20 seconds with the lid on. Add the chicken stock to create steam and cook with the lid on for 4 minutes, until tender. When ready, add the baby spinach and cook for 1 minute. Drain off any excess liquid, then transfer to a blender with the Ultratex and blitz quickly at full speed until a smooth purée forms. Adjust the seasoning, pass through a fine-meshed sieve into a bowl and cool quickly over an ice bath.

Smoked Egg Yolk

The egg yolks are heated to precisely 68ºC because at this temperature they will be lightly cooked but won't become solid or lose their bright yellow colour; instead, the liquid yolks become rich and creamy, as well as viscous enough to hold their shape when squeezed onto the plate.

    250g pasteurised egg yolks
    10ml oak-smoked water

Heat a water bath to 68ºC. Put the egg yolks in a medium sous-vide bag and seal under vacuum. Place the bag in the water bath for 30 minutes. When ready, pour the egg yolks into a bowl, stir through the smoked water and season with salt. Transfer to a squeezy bottle and keep warm until needed.

Crouton Discs

    ½ pain de mie loaf, crusts removed
    100g clarified butter
    2 garlic cloves, peeled and crushed
    2 thyme sprigs

Place the bread in the freezer for 2 hours. Put the clarified butter, garlic and thyme in a small saucepan over a medium heat until warm. Set aside to infuse for 1 hour, then pass through a fine-meshed sieve. Preheat the oven to 180ºC fan. Slice the bread on a meat slicer set to 6mm thick. Stamp out discs from the slices using a 2cm round cutter. Place a sheet of baking paper on a baking tray, brush with the infused butter, then arrange the discs on it. Brush a second sheet of baking paper with the butter and put it on top of the discs, buttered-side down. Put a heavy baking tray on top of the paper and place in the oven for 5 minutes. Transfer the baked croutons to sheets of kitchen paper and season with salt. Set aside until required.

Garlic and Parsley Butter

    Vegetable oil
    2 garlic cloves, peeled and minced
    20g banana shallots, finely diced
    30g button mushrooms, finely diced
    100g unsalted butter, softened
    10g flat-leaf parsley leaves, finely chopped
    10g ground almonds
    15g Dijon mustard
    Freshly ground white pepper

Place a heavy-based saucepan over a medium heat and add a little oil. Sauté the garlic, shallots and button mushrooms until soft, translucent and all the moisture has evaporated. Spread over a tray and allow to cool. Transfer to a bowl with the butter, parsley, almonds and mustard, season with salt and white pepper and mix thoroughly by hand. Adjust the seasoning if necessary, then transfer to a container and chill until needed.

Wild Garlic Oil

Blending the oil briefly at exactly 75ºC ensures that it captures the brightness and freshness of the chlorophyll in the wild garlic that might otherwise be lost if the oil is allowed to get too hot or the leaves sit for too long.

    250g young wild garlic leaves, washed
        and dried
    500ml grapeseed oil

Place the wild garlic in a Thermomix with 100ml of the oil and a pinch of salt, and blend to a fine paste. Add the remaining oil and blend on full speed with the heat set to 75ºC for 3 minutes. Chill in a bowl placed over an ice bath, stirring until cool. Strain the mixture through muslin, then store in a squeezy bottle until needed.

Sautéd Morels

    15ml olive oil
    40 small morels, washed and trimmed
    75ml vin jaune
    100ml Chicken Stock (see page 289)
    50g Garlic and Parsley Butter (see above)

Place a medium sauté pan over a medium–high heat. Add the oil and morels and gently sauté for 30 seconds. Season the morels with salt, then add the wine and cover with a lid. Allow to boil for 30 seconds, then add the chicken stock. Return to the boil, cover with the lid and braise over a very low heat for 6 minutes. Remove the lid, then add the garlic and parsley butter. Stir to emulsify and adjust the seasoning if necessary.

Wild Garlic Sauce

    Asparagus cooking juices, reserved from
        first step
    Wild Garlic Oil (see middle left)
    Vin jaune

Place the reserved cooking juices in a sauté pan over a medium heat and bring to the boil. Using a whisk, emulsify some wild garlic oil into the juices, and finish with a splash of vin jaune. Adjust the seasoning if necessary.

To Finish

    Raw asparagus slices
    Mustard frills
    Chickweed leaves
    Three-cornered garlic flowers
    Chive tips
    Wild Garlic Capers (see page 148)

Make 2 swipes of Asparagus Purée on each plate, then place 3 Asparagus Spears across the purée at an angle. Top with the raw asparagus slices, mustard frills, chickweed, garlic flowers, chive tips, Crouton Discs, capers and Sautéd Morels, then pipe dots of Smoked Egg Yolk around the asparagus. Serve with the warmed Wild Garlic Sauce at the table.

Slow-Cooked Hen's Egg, Celeriac, Iberico Ham, Hazelnut, Fino Sherry

Slowly cooking whole eggs at a low temperature transforms them into something really quite magical: the yolks become thick, creamy and intensely rich, and the texture of the whites becomes velvety smooth while still holding its shape. The creaminess of the eggs and accompanying celeriac purée is then offset by the salty Iberico ham, the sharpness of the lightly pickled celeriac ribbons, and the welcome crunch of the garlic chips and jamon crumb.

Serves 8

Celery Leaf Powder

100g celery leaves

Spread the leaves over a tray, then place in a dehydrator heated to 70ºC and leave for 12 hours. After the time has elapsed, transfer to a Vitamix and blitz to a powder. Keep in an airtight container until required.

Pickled Celeriac Ribbons

1 small celeriac
300ml House Pickling Liquor (see page 289)
Fine sea salt

Peel the celeriac, then use a vegetable sheeter to cut long thin sheets. Cut the sheets into ribbons about 18cm long and 3.5cm wide. Bring a large saucepan of salted water to the boil and blanch the ribbons for 10 seconds before plunging them into iced water. When cold, transfer to a container, cover with the pickling liquor and season with salt. Keep in the fridge until needed.

Celeriac Purée

1 celeriac
50g unsalted butter
200ml whole milk
200ml double cream

Peel the celeriac, then slice on a mandoline for consistently thin slices. Place a saucepan over a medium heat and add the butter. When foaming, add the celeriac slices, season with salt and sweat without colouring for 2 minutes. Now cover with the milk and cream, bring to the boil and simmer for 30 minutes, until tender. Drain, reserving the liquid for blending. Transfer the celeriac to a Vitamix and blend, adding a little of the cooking liquid if needed. Adjust the seasoning if necessary.

Fino Sherry Velouté

100g carrots, peeled
100g shallots, peeled
50g button mushrooms
100g unsalted butter
500ml Chicken Stock (see page 289)
400ml fino sherry
200ml double cream

Finely slice the carrots, shallots and mushrooms. Put the butter into a large, heavy-based saucepan and place over a medium heat. Add the carrots, shallots and mushrooms, season with salt and sweat for 10 minutes, until sweet and tender. Add the stock to the pan and allow to reduce by half. Pour in 200ml of the fino sherry and reduce by half. Add the cream and bring to the boil. Allow to simmer for 2 minutes, then set aside to infuse for 20 minutes. Add the remaining fino sherry, season with salt and pass through a fine-meshed chinois.

Iberico Ham Crumb

100g Iberico ham trimmings, excess fat removed
20ml vegetable oil

Dice the ham into small pieces. Place a frying pan over a medium heat and add the oil. When warm, add the ham and cook until it starts to bubble and crisp up. Keep stirring so it fries evenly and doesn't catch on the bottom of the pan. Strain off the cooking oil and place the ham on a tray lined with kitchen paper. Transfer to a dehydrator heated to 70ºC and leave for 4 hours, until completely dry. After the time has elapsed, finely chop the ham to a crumb texture. Reserve in an airtight container until needed.

Garlic Chips

Cooking the garlic slices in milk three times before frying them removes some of their heat and pungency, leaving a sweeter, more mellow flavour that complements the other ingredients rather than overwhelming them.

3 elephant garlic cloves
300ml whole milk
200ml vegetable oil

Peel the garlic and finely slice on a mandoline. Put the garlic slices and 100ml of the milk into a small saucepan over a medium heat and bring to the boil. Strain, discarding the milk, then repeat this process twice more. Next, dry the garlic slices on kitchen paper. Pour the oil into a small sauté pan over a medium–high heat and bring up to 150ºC. Add the garlic and fry until golden brown. Drain on kitchen paper and season with salt. Allow to cool and put to one side for later.

Slow-Cooked Hen's Egg

8 free-range eggs, at room temperature

Heat a water bath to 63ºC, then add the whole eggs and cook for 40 minutes. Remove from the water bath and keep warm.

To Finish

Iberico ham slices
Toasted hazelnuts, halved
Celery leaves
Mustard leaves
Chickweed leaves
Three-cornered leek flowers
Freshly ground mignonette pepper

Place a large spoonful of warmed Celeriac Purée in the middle of a bowl and create a well in the middle. Sprinkle the purée with the Iberico Ham Crumb. Peel the Slow-Cooked Hen's Eggs, then place one in the purée well and season with salt and mignonette pepper. Sprinkle one side of the Pickled Celeriac Ribbons with Celery Leaf Powder before rolling into rosettes. Arrange the ham slices and celeriac rosettes around the egg, then garnish with the toasted hazelnuts, Garlic Chips, leaves and flowers. Warm the Fino Sherry Velouté and aerate with a hand-held blender before serving it in a jug on the side.

Isle of Skye Scallops, Ajo Blanco, Verjus, Olive Oil

Isle of Skye scallops are celebrated for their size and sweetness, and although we serve them with creamy ajo blanco, sweet but acidic grapes and sharp hits of verjus gel, it is definitely the scallops that take centre stage here. Once they have been removed from the shell, the scallops are simply sautéd, then brushed with a little miso glaze before serving. This dish is a great example of our philosophy at Restaurant Gordon Ramsay, where we source the best ingredients possible and let them shine.

Serves 8

Ajo Blanco

Ajo blanco means 'white garlic' in Spain, where this cold soup originates. It is traditionally made with almonds, but we use macadamia nuts for their rich, buttery flavour and creamy texture. Freezing the ajo blanco and churning it three times makes it incredibly smooth.

    1 garlic clove, peeled
    300ml Vegetable Nage (see page 289)
    200g macadamia nuts
    10g fine sea salt
    10ml sherry vinegar
    15ml Colombino extra virgin olive oil

Put the garlic into a small saucepan and cover with cold water. Place the pan over a medium–high heat and bring to the boil. Repeat this process twice more, then place the garlic clove in a Vitamix with the vegetable nage, macadamia nuts, salt, sherry vinegar and olive oil. Blend on full speed until smooth, then transfer to a Pacojet beaker and freeze. Once frozen, churn and refreeze twice more, then store in the fridge until needed.

Miso Glaze

    110g white miso
    30g caster sugar
    1 tbsp mirin
    1 tbsp sake
    1 tsp soy sauce

Combine all the ingredients in a saucepan and place over a medium–high heat. Bring to the boil, then put to one side until required.

Verjus Gel

    300ml verjus
    100g Stock Syrup (see page 290)
    12g agar agar

Pour the verjus, stock syrup and 200ml water into a saucepan over a medium heat, whisk in the agar agar and bring to the boil for 2 minutes. Pour into a tray and place in the fridge to set. Once set, transfer the gel to a Vitamix and blend until smooth. Pass through a fine-meshed drum sieve, then pour into a squeezy bottle for service.

Scallop Preparation

    8 extra large scallops

To shuck the scallops, take a knife with a long, narrow blade similar to a boning knife and carefully insert it between the two sides of the shell close to where they join. Keep the blade angled towards the flat shell and make one slice down in a sweeping motion; this will free the flat shell, which can now be discarded. Use the tip of the knife to carefully cut the semi-translucent muscle from between the white scallop meat and the shell – this will free the scallop. Next, carefully slide a thumb between the muscle and the scallop meat to remove the skirt and roe. Wash the scallops gently in iced water and place on kitchen paper until needed.

To Finish

    Vegetable oil
    Peeled green grapes
    Sliced black grapes
    Salty fingers (or samphire)
    Chervil frond
    Dill frond
    Chive tips
    Colombino extra virgin olive oil
    Fine sea salt

Place a large, non-stick frying pan over a high heat. Slice each prepared Scallop from top to bottom into 3 evenly sized pieces and lightly season with salt. Pour a little vegetable oil into the frying pan, add your scallops and allow them to cook until golden brown. Once caramelised, flip them over for 10 seconds, then remove from the pan. Next, brush a little of the Miso Glaze over the scallop slices and arrange on plates. Place dots of the Verjus Gel around the scallops, followed by the grapes and salty fingers. Carefully arrange the herbs on top. Gently warm the Ajo Blanco in a small saucepan and place 2 spoonfuls next to the scallops. Drizzle a little Colombino olive oil over the ajo blanco at the table.

Sea-Trout 'Escabeche', Carrot, Saffron, Sauternes

Both the flavours and the colours of this dish work together beautifully, the orange of the fish being exactly the same hue as the carrot purée and marinated salmon roe it is served with. The lightly treated sea trout is full of flavour, which is augmented by the citrus cure used in the brine and the lemon oil it is very gently 'cooked' in. A stunning carrot, Sauternes and saffron dressing then brings everything together at the table.

Serves 8

Citrus Cure

250g Maldon sea salt
250g caster sugar
Zest of 2 pink grapefruits
Zest of 4 lemons
10g toasted coriander seeds

Pour the salt and sugar into a Thermomix with the citrus zest and coriander seeds and blend for 20 seconds, until thoroughly incorporated. Store in an airtight container until needed.

Lemon Oil

Peel of 3 lemons
1 litre pomace oil

Heat a water bath to 70°C. Make sure there is no pith on the lemon peel, then place it in a sous-vide bag with the pomace oil. Seal the bag under vacuum and place it in the water bath for 3 hours. After the time has elapsed, remove the bag from the bath and allow to cool in the fridge overnight, then strain and store in the fridge until needed.

Pickled Carrot Ribbons

2 large orange carrots
2 large yellow carrots
2 large purple carrots
300ml House Pickling Liquor (see page 289)

Peel the carrots and cut into pieces 7cm long. Using a mandoline, carefully slice the pieces lengthways into strips 1mm thick. Once all sliced, make sure each strip is 2cm wide and 7cm long, trimming off any excess. Put the pickling liquor into a small saucepan and bring to the boil over a medium–high heat. Place the different coloured carrots in 3 separate bowls and cover each one with a third of the pickling liquor. When required, drain the pickling liquor and roll the carrots into cylinders.

Carrot, Sauternes and Saffron Dressing

1 litre carrot juice
100ml Sauternes
15ml Saffron Water (see page 290)
25ml chardonnay vinegar
50ml extra virgin olive oil
Fine sea salt

Pour the carrot juice and Sauternes into a saucepan and add the saffron water and chardonnay vinegar. Place the pan over a medium heat and allow to reduce to a light glaze. Season with salt and adjust the acidity if required. Split with the olive oil and store until needed.

Baby Fennel

8 baby fennel bulbs

Bring a small saucepan of salted water to the boil. Carefully trim off the fennel roots, then cut the bulbs into diagonal slices 5cm long, saving the leafy tops for the garnish. Blanch the fennel in the boiling water for 3 minutes, then refresh in iced water for 5 minutes. Once cooled, drain on kitchen paper and cut in half lengthways. Store until needed.

Carrot Purée

Sand carrots are so called because they are grown in extremely sandy soil by the Normandy coast in northern France. Not only are sandy conditions particularly good for growing this particularly delicious variety, but the sand also helps the carrots to preserve their flavour after they are picked.

500g sand carrots, peeled and sliced
250g sand carrots, peeled and juiced

Put the carrot slices into a saucepan with the carrot juice and season with salt. Cover with a lid and cook over a medium heat for about 20 minutes, until the carrots are soft and most of the juice has reduced. Once soft, transfer to a Vitamix and blend until smooth. Adjust the seasoning if necessary.

Marinated Trout Roe

25ml soy sauce
25ml mirin
25ml sake
50g trout roe

Mix the soy, mirin and sake together. Gently mix in the trout roe and leave to marinate for 20 minutes. Once the time has elapsed, pass the roe through a small fine-meshed sieve and store until needed.

Sea-Trout

Brining the fish in the dissolved citrus cure before cooking it not only adds flavour from the grapefruit and lemon zest and seasoning from the salt, it also improves the texture of the sea-trout and helps it to hold its shape during the cooking and resting process.

1 × 3kg sea-trout, filleted
200g Citrus Cure (see far left)
300ml Lemon Oil (see far left)

Pin-bone and skin the trout fillets, then remove the bloodline. Trim off the thin side of the fillets, keeping the large eye of the loin, then remove the less thick tail end of the fillets. Make a 10% brine by dissolving the citrus cure in 2 litres water. Place the trout in the brine for 20 minutes, then drain and dry thoroughly. Put the fillets into individual sous-vide bags with 150ml lemon oil and seal under vacuum. Heat a water bath to 40°C and place the bags in it for 20 minutes. When ready, chill in an ice bath. Once cold, remove from the sous-vide bags and dry with kitchen paper, then wrap tightly with cling film and leave to rest for a minimum of 6 hours.

To Finish

Pickled Shallot Rings (see page 149)
Toasted coriander seeds
Red-veined sorrel leaves
Oxalis leaves
Nasturtium leaves
Dill fronds
Fennel flowers

Remove the Sea-trout fillets from the cling film and slice into smaller bars 2.5cm wide. Put 3 pieces of trout onto each plate and sprinkle with a little flaky sea salt. Arrange the Pickled Carrot Ribbons and Baby Fennel slices on the plates, then place various-sized dots of Carrot Purée around them. Place 3 small spoonfuls of Marinated Trout Roe on the plate, and finally garnish with the pickled shallot rings, coriander seeds, herbs and flowers. Serve the Carrot, Sauternes and Saffron Dressing on the side.

NOT A MOMENT TOO SOON

The year 2000 was the longest year of my life. I'd been racing to take the restaurant to three Michelin stars and fell at the final hurdle. I was bitterly disappointed, but there's no point looking back. I'd accepted the verdict and in some ways that disappointment, that pressure on my shoulders, helped sharpen my resolve and distil the team's focus. We continued what we were doing, getting incrementally better every day. Refining, redefining and staying true to ourselves and our DNA to deliver the perfect experience for every diner. Nothing left that kitchen unless it was perfect.

I developed the eye of a hawk, seeing every minuscule detail from a distance, and my team followed suit. We became a high-functioning machine working in rhythm, and we were at the peak of our game. The back and front of house were in sync and communicating without words, dancing to the same beat. It was beautiful.

A restaurant takes time to grow into its body, to put meat on its bones. When a restaurant finds its rhythm it's a spectacular thing to experience as a guest. You can feel the energy, that magic, the moment you walk through the door.

It sounds a bit ludicrous now, but after failing to capture a third star, I felt I couldn't take any chances. To succeed the following year I had to block out all external distractions and keep my eye on the ball, ready for the moment a Michelin inspector walked through the door again.

That moment came in early 2001, and I've relived it over and over. I'd attributed so much importance to it that it felt like the longest and most gruelling service I had ever done. The restaurant was packed. The team was working smoothly, but we were hyper-aware, almost as if things were happening in super-slow motion.

The editor of *The Michelin Guide*, Derek Brown, and the number one Michelin inspector, Derek Bulmer, arrived for dinner – the two most important Dereks I'd ever meet.

Their order came through and I remember it to this day: one lobster ravioli, one scallop, one pigeon, one sea bass, one fondant and one raspberry soufflé. But then that two top (table for two) turned into a four top (table for four) because they wanted doubles of everything so they could both try every dish.

We started them off with a wonderful slow-roasted pumpkin velouté with a dusting of caramelised cep powder as a little amuse-bouche.

To drink, they ordered a bloody Mary and a glass of champagne, then two whites and two reds. I was desperate to send them more food. It's such an unnerving feeling when inspectors are in the house. I had this kitchen full of goodies and was tempted to slip in another course, but I knew deep down that doing so would be catastrophic.

I went into the dining room to say hello to a table of regulars and I will never forget it. The Michelin judges were on table five, and the regulars on table three, just beside them. I glanced over the whole room and said good evening to everyone in one breath, but didn't engage with anybody apart from the regulars on table three. I was trying to be as normal as possible, but I was sweating bullets. I couldn't stop thinking 'I'm cooking the biggest, most important dinner of my career; do I dare talk to the inspectors?'

In my head it felt like a World Cup final that's just gone into extra time. I knew we were headed for a penalty shoot-out, so I went back into the kitchen to play my best game.

By 10.30pm we were coming to the end of the three-and-a-half-hour service. The dining room started to empty out and Jean-Claude came through to the kitchen and said table five would like a word. It was penalty shoot-out time.

'Can you send them through to the bar for a drink, and I'll come out and join them?'

If I was about to receive bad news, I didn't want it to be in the dining room in front of staff and the remaining guests because I didn't know how I'd react if the news was grim. On the other hand, if it was good news, I wanted to be the one to tell the staff myself.

I asked the two kitchen porters to start polishing glasses because I didn't want any clutter in the bar. When you sit with highly respected people in the industry and you hear a plate or glass smash, there is simply nothing worse. So I set up this chat in the bar like it was D-Day.

While Jean-Claude gave the inspectors another espresso and some more petit fours, I raced downstairs and grabbed a brand new super-starched apron, raced back upstairs, paused at the kitchen door, took a deep breath and walked into the bar.

'Mr Bulmer, Mr Brown, really nice to see you,' I said, as I shook hands and sat down.

You never ask an inspector 'How was it?' That's the worst thing you could ever ask because if it wasn't perfect, you should not have sent it out to them in the first place. Once again, I felt like everything was happening in slow motion. My throat was dry and I didn't know what to say, so it was a relief when they asked how Christmas was and how my family were, though I was actually thinking, 'Please, just get to it.'

This was ten days before the guide was coming out, but it still hadn't dawned on me that it was already written. The inspectors must have already been in to review things and I'd not realised when that was. In that case, what the hell were they doing here? My stomach was in knots, my mouth as dry as a desert, and I was praying for someone to put me out of my misery. But still I had to wait as they began to discuss and deconstruct the meal they'd just had, particularly the lightness of the raspberry soufflé.

Then there was an awkward silence. They both looked around to make sure no one was in the dining room. They had been waiting for the last tables to leave, but I was so caught up in this bubble that I didn't even realise that had happened.

I'll never forget the words: 'Gordon, in the forthcoming Michelin guide out in ten days' time, we're happy to award you three stars.'

I nearly burst into tears, but I didn't want to do that in front of them. I was lost for words and couldn't think how to react so I got up and hugged them.

I sat back down, but felt like I was floating. I had this strange weightlessness. There are only a few hundred chefs on the planet ever to experience a moment like this. I'd dreamed of it all my career and now I was in that dream for real. Everything that had happened up to that point – the sacrifices, such as having to sell our home and rent an apartment, having to walk to work because I couldn't afford a car, not taking a salary because I wanted to employ more staff, the long hours – they had all been worth it. I always get emotional about the moment I heard the verdict because it was everything up to that point in my life distilled into one sentence.

'You're the only one,' they continued.

'What do you mean?' I asked.

'The only one in London this year to have three Michelin stars awarded.'

It's one of the few times in my life I've been rendered speechless. Thankfully, they had more talking to do. They were awed at the level of consistency and made a point of revealing how many times they'd been to the restaurant without us knowing. With, I might add, a representative from nearly every country in Europe paying us a visit. They explained that one of the real highlights as an inspector is watching young talent rise to the top. They'd seen me with two stars at Aubergine when I was 27 and watched my progression to three stars at Restaurant Gordon Ramsay.

They also talked about my heritage and how exciting it was to see a Scottish chef rise to the top. While I was born in Scotland, I never wanted to play the Scottish card; I just wanted to be the best chef I could. But I know that Scottishness is at my core, even though I grew up in Stratford-upon-Avon. I have a lot of family still in Scotland, and in the restaurant we use lots of ingredients from Scotland because they are stunningly good.

The inspectors gave me a copy of the new guide, and it felt like I was given the power to fly. When leaving, they said, 'Don't call a cab, we're going to walk to Sloane Square and enjoy the moment.'

I raced into the kitchen where all the staff were waiting in anticipation and let out this almighty scream. And the team went crazy. It was the most joyous release of tension imaginable – like winning the World Cup with the last kick of a penalty shoot-out. We opened four bottles of Dom Pérignon and had a hell of a party.

Winning that third star was everything I ever wanted, everything I ever needed as a chef. I had ticked the biggest box of all. After all the shit I had taken – the bullets from Marco, the potatoes thrown by Joël Robuchon, the screaming from Guy Savoy in response to my cock-ups – everything suddenly made sense. All that learning and experience funnelled into this moment. It had paid off.

Being awarded three stars gave me permission to move to the next stage – to teach and delegate, to let the restaurant continue to evolve and set the standard, but also allowed me to climb new mountains. You can't ever think the job is done and roll up your knives and go home. The hardest thing now was maintaining that level. I had to watch more and do less. Work *on* the restaurant, not necessarily *in* it.

I needed to elevate and enhance the individuals around me and give them as much opportunity as I had enjoyed myself. Let them thrive and give them inspiration, and create paths for their aspirations.

The night of the champagne celebration Jean-Claude said to me, 'Where do we go from here?'

'We go for four stars,' I replied.

'What?' he exclaimed. 'There's no such thing.'

'Exactly. But that will be our focus.'

Cornish Cod, Jersey Royals, Morels, Vin Jaune

Land and sea combine in this dish of Cornish cod with new-season Jersey Royals and morels. The slight saltiness of the tiny potatoes and the gently brined fish work so well with the earthiness of the mushrooms and the bright green flavours of the herb purée, a combination echoed by the crisp potato and kombu crumb that tops the fish – it is both earthy and briny at the same time, and adds a lovely texture to the flaky cod.

Serves 8

Cod

    1 × 7kg cod, filleted
    100g fine sea salt

Remove the skin from the cod. Trim off the thin side of the fillets and the small top muscle, keeping the large eye of the loin, then remove the less thick tail end of the fillets. Make a 10% brine by mixing the salt with 1 litre water, making sure the salt dissolves completely. Put the fillets into the brine for 10 minutes. Lift them out and wrap in kitchen paper to dry for 10 minutes. Once dry, wrap the fillets separately in cling film to form ballotines, then place in the fridge for 12 hours. Portion the fillets, then remove the cling film and keep in the fridge until needed.

Vin Jaune Sabayon

A sabayon is a custard-like sauce usually made with sugar and Marsala, and served as or with a dessert. A savoury sabayon lacks the sugar, but is still rich and creamy, with a sharpness that makes it an excellent accompaniment to fish and shellfish.

For the Reduction
    100g shallots, peeled and finely sliced
    200ml vin jaune
    1 thyme sprig
    1 garlic clove, cracked with the blade
        of a chef's knife
    5 white peppercorns

For the Sabayon
    20ml Vin Jaune Reduction (see above)
    10g lemon juice
    100ml Vegetable Nage (see page 289)
    50ml vin jaune
    85g pasteurised egg yolks
    150ml extra virgin olive oil
    6g fine sea salt

To make the reduction, put the shallots, vin jaune, thyme, garlic and peppercorns into a saucepan and bring to the boil. Reduce by half, then remove from the heat and allow to cool. Pass through a fine-meshed sieve.

Combine all the sabayon ingredients in a bowl, then pour into a sous-vide bag and seal under vacuum. Heat a water bath to 75°C and place the bag in it for 30 minutes. Decant into a 1-litre siphon loaded with a single nitrous oxide charge, and keep in a water bath heated to 50°C until needed.

Smoked Jersey Royals

    100g Jersey Royal potatoes
    50g unsalted butter
    5ml oak-smoked water
    2g fine sea salt

Thoroughly wash the potatoes. Place them in a sous-vide bag with the butter, smoked water and salt and seal under vacuum. Heat a water bath to 95°C and place the bag in it for 30 minutes. When ready, cool in an ice bath.

Herb Purée

    100g lovage
    100g flat-leaf parsley
    100g mint, leaves picked
    100g chervil
    100g dill
    100g basil
    100g fennel fronds
    10g fine sea salt
    50ml Colombino extra virgin olive oil
    20g Ultratex

Keeping the hard and soft herbs separate, pick the leaves and discard the stalks (they can be reserved for the vegetable nage needed in the Sabayon, left). Bring a large saucepan of water to the boil, add the hard herbs for 4 minutes, then add the soft herbs for 2 minutes. Drain thoroughly, squeezing out any excess water, then put the herbs into a Vitamix, season with the salt and blitz together. With the blender running, slowly pour in the olive oil, then add the Ultratex and blend for 2 minutes, until smooth. Cool over an ice bath. Once cool, transfer to a Pacojet beaker and freeze. When frozen, blitz in the Pacojet, refreeze and repeat this step twice more. Transfer the purée to a squeezy bottle and store in the fridge until needed.

Potato and Salted Kombu Crumb

It is essential to remove the starch from the potato by washing it thoroughly, and then to dry it completely by straining through muslin, otherwise the flesh will be wet and gluey rather than light, crisp and fluffy as desired.

    1 large King Edward potato
    400ml vegetable oil
    50g salted kombu, finely chopped
    Fine sea salt

Peel the potato and roughly chop. Place in a Thermomix, cover with water and blend at full speed for 10 seconds. Pass through a fine-meshed chinois and rinse off all the starchy water for 5 minutes. Allow to drip-dry for 10 minutes in a fine-meshed chinois. Place the potato pulp in a saucepan and add the vegetable oil. Whisk until combined, then place the pan over a medium heat and cook gently until the potato is golden and crispy. Drain off the oil and transfer the crumb to kitchen paper to drain further. When drained, mix the potato crumb with the kombu and season with salt if required.

To Finish

    1kg Beurre Noisette (see page 289)
    Vegetable oil
    Sautéd Morels (see page 59)
    Winter purslane leaves
    Pink purslane leaves
    Pennywort leaves
    Chickweed leaves
    Chive tips
    Chive flowers

Put the beurre noisette into a medium sauté pan and warm to 55°C. Place a frying pan over a high heat, add a little vegetable oil and sear off one side of the Cod portions. Next, place the cod in the melted beurre noisette to confit for around 8–10 minutes. When cooked, cover the caramelised surface with the Potato and Salted Kombu Crumb. Reheat the Smoked Jersey Royals and cook the morels. Place the cod in the middle of a plate and arrange the smoked potatoes and sautéd morels around the left-hand side of the fish. Place dots of Herb Purée around the edges and garnish with the herb leaves and flowers. Siphon the warm Vin Jaune Sabayon into a sauce jug and serve on the side.

Pigeon, Almond, Apricot, Fennel

The breasts of the pigeon are pan-roasted until perfectly pink, then glazed with honey and soy, while the legs are cooked very slowly in duck fat until the meat is falling from the bone, then coated in puffed amaranth seeds and toasted almonds. Both cuts of meat bring something different to this elegant dish and are balanced by the wonderful combination of apricots, carrots and fresh green almonds, then finished with an intense spiced pigeon sauce that is served at the table.

Serves 8

Pigeon Preparation

4 × 500g pigeons

Using a cleaver or similar knife, remove the pigeon wings at the joint, saving them for the pigeon sauce (right). Next, cut off and discard the head, leaving the neck as long as possible. Roll the pigeon over so that the breasts are facing down and make an incision along the middle of the neck to split the skin from it. Carefully remove the neck and any excess fat, being careful not to tear the skin. Now cut off the neck bone as close to the breasts as possible and keep it for the sauce. Next, remove the legs and set them aside for the confit process. Make a small cut behind the point of the breasts, then separate the guts and rear end from the crown. Remove and discard all the innards, but keep the bones for the sauce. Set the crown aside to be cooked later.

Confit Pigeon Legs

8 pigeon legs
100g fine sea salt
1 thyme sprig
1 garlic clove, cracked with the blade of a chef's knife
50g duck fat

Using scissors, cut the feet off the pigeon legs. Scrape the meat from the thigh bone with a small knife, until you can see the bone – this makes it easier to remove after cooking. Toss the legs with the salt until they are generously covered, then chill for 1 hour. After the time has elapsed, rinse well and pat dry. Place the legs flat and spaced apart in a sous-vide bag with the thyme, garlic and duck fat and seal under vacuum. Heat a water bath to 85°C and place the bag in it for 4 hours. Transfer the bag to an ice bath to cool. Once cold, use scissors to remove the thigh bones, reserving them for the pigeon sauce, and French-trim the ankle bone. Set aside until needed.

Spiced Pigeon Sauce

6g coriander seeds
2g cardamom seeds
1 cinnamon stick
2 star anise
10 black peppercorns
2g juniper berries
2 cloves
Vegetable oil
Pigeon bones, reserved from initial preparation and confit, chopped
3 shallots, peeled and sliced
2 thyme sprigs
½ bay leaf
2 garlic cloves, cracked with the blade of a chef's knife
50ml sherry vinegar
750ml ruby port
1 litre Veal Stock (see page 289)
1 litre Chicken Stock (see page 289)
Fine sea salt

Crush all the spices using a pestle and mortar. Place a large, heavy-based saucepan over a high heat. Add some oil and start to caramelise the bones. Once they are roasted, season with salt. Add the shallots, thyme, bay leaf, garlic and crushed spices to the pan with a little more oil and sweat until soft. Add the sherry vinegar and allow to reduce to a glaze over a high heat. Next, add the ruby port and again reduce to a glaze. Once the port has reduced, add the stocks, bring to the boil, then simmer for around 45 minutes, skimming regularly, until reduced to a sauce consistency. Strain through a fine-meshed chinois, adjust the seasoning if necessary and set aside until needed.

Apricot Gastrique

A gastrique is a very simple sweet-and-sour sauce made from reduced sugar and vinegar, and sometimes flavoured with fruit, in this case apricot purée. It is used to add depth and contrast to sauces, and to impart flavour and balance when cooking vegetables, like the baby fennel used to finish the dish.

250g Boiron apricot purée
125g caster sugar
125ml champagne vinegar

Put the purée, sugar and vinegar into a saucepan with 250ml water and place over a medium–high heat. Allow to reduce to a thick syrup.

Apricot Gel

500g Boiron apricot purée
25ml chardonnay vinegar
25ml crème d'abricot liqueur
6g agar agar

Place the apricot purée, vinegar and liqueur in a saucepan over a medium heat, whisk in the agar agar and bring to the boil for 2 minutes. Pour into a tray and place in the fridge to set. Once set, transfer the gel to a Vitamix and blend until smooth. Pass through a fine-meshed drum sieve, then pour into a squeezy bottle for service.

Almond Cream

1 litre whole milk
250ml double cream
125g ground almonds
75ml Amaretto
25ml orgeat syrup
1% Gellan F

Put the milk and cream into a saucepan and place over a medium–high heat. Bring to the boil, then remove from the heat and whisk in the ground almonds. Season with a pinch of salt, then cover the pan with cling film and allow to infuse for 30 minutes. Strain into a bowl, squeezing all the liquid out of the almonds. Add the Amaretto and orgeat syrup and adjust the seasoning, if required. Weigh the liquid to calculate 1% of it, and add that amount of Gellan F. Blend in a Thermomix at 95°C for 1 minute, then transfer to a chilled tray and allow to set in the fridge. Once set, blend again in the Thermomix at 50°C to achieve a smooth purée. Pass through a fine-meshed drum sieve and set aside until needed.

Cooking the Pigeon

Vegetable oil
4 prepared pigeon crowns (see first step,
    opposite)
Unsalted butter
1 thyme sprig
1 garlic clove, cracked with the blade
    of a chef's knife

Place a heavy-based frying pan, preferably
cast iron, over a medium heat and add a little
oil. Season the pigeon with salt, then place
it in the pan, one breast side down, and allow
to colour. Once coloured, turn over and repeat
on the other breast. Now stand the crown up
and allow the bottom of it to colour. Add a knob
of butter, the thyme sprig and garlic clove
and baste the pigeon with the foaming butter.
Be careful not to let the butter burn. Next,
turn the crown up onto the breasts and baste
the inside of the cavity for 30 seconds. Turn
the bird back over for a further 2 minutes, and
continue to baste. It will take approximately
10 minutes to pan-fry the pigeon, depending
on size. To test whether it is cooked, squeeze
the breast near the wings – it should give
medium resistance. Once cooked, remove
the crown from the pan and allow it to rest
for 10 minutes.

Cooking the Confit Pigeon Legs

Vegetable oil
8 Confit Pigeon Legs (see second step,
    opposite)
50ml Honey Glaze (see page 127)
50g toasted nibbed almonds
25g puffed amaranth seeds

Place a little more oil in the empty pigeon
pan and fry the Confit pigeon legs over a
medium heat until the skin is crispy and the
meat has warmed through. Glaze the skin
with the honey glaze, then coat in the nibbed
almonds and amaranth. Place 5 small dots
of apricot purée on each leg and garnish
with some of the finishing fronds and herbs.

To Finish

Baby Fennel (see page 70)
Apricot wedges
Green almonds, shelled and peeled
Fennel fronds
Sweet cicely
Fennel flowers
Coriander flowers

Remove the Pigeon breasts from the crowns.
French-trim around the remaining wing bones,
then glaze the skin with the remaining honey
glaze. Warm the baby fennel in 50ml of the
Apricot Gastrique. Arrange the apricot wedges,
fennel slices and peeled almonds on the plate,
followed by the Apricot Gel and Almond Cream
in various-sized dots. Add the remaining fronds,
leaves and flowers, and finally place the breast
on the plate. Serve with a pan-fried Confit
Pigeon Leg and the warmed Spiced Pigeon
Sauce on the side.

Guinea Fowl 'Blanquette', Alliums, Vin Jaune, Jus Gras

We take our inspiration for this dish from the traditional flavours and creaminess of a classic French blanquette, or white stew, and then thicken it to create this eye-catching presentation for guinea fowl. Served with four different types of onions prepared in contrasting ways, and garnished with delicate herbs and seasonal flowers, this tastes as stunning as it looks.

Serves 8

Smoked Onion Petals

10 baby onions, peeled and halved
100ml House Pickling Liquor (see page 289)
50ml oak-smoked water
35ml Stock Syrup (see page 290)

Put the onion halves into a sous-vide bag with the pickling liquor, smoked water and stock syrup. Seal under vacuum and leave to marinate for 48 hours in the fridge. When the time has elapsed, heat a water bath to 95°C and place the bag in it for 30 minutes. Transfer to an ice bath to chill. Once chilled, separate the onions into individual petals and store in the cooking liquor until needed.

Guinea Fowl

4 guinea fowl
500g fine sea salt
300ml Chicken Stock (see page 289)
8 thyme sprigs
4 garlic cloves, cracked with the blade of a chef's knife
100g unsalted butter

Remove the legs and wings from the guinea fowl, reserving them for sauce another time. Make a 10% brine by dissolving the salt in 5 litres of water. Put the guinea fowl crowns into the brine for 1 hour. Heat a water bath to 65°C. Put the crowns into individual sous-vide bags with a ladleful of chicken stock, a sprig of thyme and a clove of garlic, then seal under vacuum. Place the bags in the water bath for 50 minutes. Transfer to an ice bath to chill. When cold, remove each breast carefully from the crown and take off the skin, trimming any sinews. Place each breast in a sous-vide bag with a small slice of butter and a sprig of thyme. Seal under vacuum and keep chilled until needed.

Vin Jaune 'Blanquette'

We add the thickening agent Gellan F to the creamy blanquette sauce so that it coats the guinea fowl breasts perfectly every time. As Gellan gum has a high melting point, it won't break down – in the way that gelatine and agar agar would – when the sauce is heated.

200g carrots, peeled
50g button mushroom
175g unsalted butter
1 litre Chicken Stock (see page 289)
350ml vin jaune
350ml double cream
10g Gellan F
Fine sea salt

Finely slice the carrots and mushrooms. Put the butter into a large, heavy-based saucepan and place over a medium heat. Add the carrots and mushrooms, season and sweat for 20 minutes, until sweet and tender. Add the stock to the pan and allow to reduce by half. Pour in 100ml of the vin jaune and reduce by half. Add the cream and bring to the boil. Allow to simmer for 5 minutes, then set aside to infuse for 20 minutes. Add the remaining vin jaune, season with salt and pass through a fine-meshed sieve. Pour 1 litre of the sauce into a Thermomix, heat to 90°C, then add the Gellan F and blend on full speed for 2 minutes. Pour into a tray and place in the blast chiller to set. Once set, blend in the Thermomix until smooth. Adjust the seasoning, if necessary, and transfer to a squeezy bottle. Keep warm until needed.

Onion Purée

500g onions, peeled and finely sliced
50ml double cream
1% Gellan F

Place the onions in a bowl, season with salt, then place in a medium sous-vide bag and seal under vacuum. Place a large saucepan of water over a high heat and bring to a simmer. Place the bag in the water and cook for 1 hour, until the onions are tender. When ready, transfer them to a Thermomix and add the cream. Blend until smooth, then weigh the purée to calculate 1% of it, and add that amount of the Gellan F. Bring the temperature of the purée up to 90°C, add the Gellan and blend on full speed for 2 minutes. Pour the purée into a clean tray and leave to set in a blast chiller. Once set, return to the Thermomix, blend until smooth and adjust the seasoning if necessary. Place in a squeezy bottle until needed.

To Finish

White garlic buds
Brassica buds
Purple allium buds
Thyme leaves
Chive batons
Spring onion roundels
Grilled grelot onions
Lettuce spears
Golden purslane leaves
Mustard frills
Brassica flowers
Pink garlic flowers
Jus Gras (see page 257)

To cook the Guinea Fowl, heat a water bath to 65°C degrees and place the sous-vide bags containing the breasts in it for 10 minutes. Remove from the bags and coat with the warm Vin Jaune Blanquette. Garnish the breasts with the flower buds, thyme leaves, chive batons and spring onion roundels, and place them on plates. Arrange the grilled grelots in a line alongside the breasts, add dots of the Onion Purée, then add the Smoked Onion Petals. Finish with the lettuce spears, golden purslane, mustard frills, brassica flowers and pink garlic flowers. Serve the jus gras on the side.

Dexter Beef Short Rib, Smoked Bone Marrow, Peas, Baby Onions

Slow-cooked Dexter beef provides a rich and savoury backdrop for the vibrant flavours of fresh peas and sweet baby onions. Adding bone marrow to the sauce makes it even more rich and unctuous, and it finishes this often overlooked but always exceptional cut of beef in a very satisfying and indulgent way.

Serves 8

Dexter Beef Short Rib

Cooking the beef at a low temperature for such a long time means the connective tissue in it completely breaks down without losing any moisture. The result is soft, melt-in-the-mouth meat that offers almost no resistance.

  2 × 3-bone short ribs
  200g rendered beef fat
  Fine sea salt and freshly ground
     black pepper

Remove the bones from the beef, then season the meat with salt and black pepper. Blowtorch all the beef to quickly seal it without cooking it. Place each piece of beef in a sous-vide bag with half the beef fat and seal under vacuum. Heat a water bath to 58°C and place the bag in it for 48 hours. When the time has elapsed, remove the bag from the water and chill in an ice bath. Keep in the fridge until needed.

Smoked Bone Marrow

Once it has been extracted from the bone, the bone marrow has to be soaked for at least 24 hours to remove any blood or bacteria. This process also improves its colour and texture.

  200g bone marrow, removed from the bone
  100g smoking chips

Soak the bone marrow in cold water, changing the water regularly until the marrow is white (this process can take a few days). Set up a smoking station by placing a wire cake rack on top of a roasting tray. Put the wood chips into a saucepan over a high heat until they begin to smoke. Transfer the smoking chips to the roasting tray and place the bone marrow on the wire rack above them. Set the chips on fire using a blowtorch, then quickly cover the dish with foil and smoke the bone marrow for 10 minutes. Transfer to the fridge to cool. Once cool, dice the marrow using a hot knife, which will make it easier to cut. Store in the fridge until needed.

Beef Sauce

  100ml vegetable oil
  1.5kg beef trimmings
  3 shallots, peeled and sliced
  3 garlic cloves, cracked with the blade
     of a chef's knife
  10 black peppercorns
  1 thyme sprig
  ½ bay leaf
  50ml cabernet sauvignon vinegar
  350ml brandy
  750ml red wine
  1 litre Veal Stock (see page 289)
  1 litre Chicken Stock (see page 289)

Place a large, heavy-based saucepan over a medium–high heat and add the oil. When hot, add the beef trimmings and cook until browned all over. Add the shallots, garlic and peppercorns and continue to cook for 2 minutes. Next, add the thyme and bay leaf, then deglaze the pan with the vinegar, add the brandy and reduce to a glaze. Pour in the red wine and reduce to a glaze again. Once reduced, add the stocks and bring to the boil. Reduce the heat and simmer for 1 hour, removing any scum from the surface and keeping the side of the pan brushed down. Once cooked, pass through a fine-meshed chinois lined with muslin. Adjust the seasoning if necessary, then cool and put to one side until needed.

Pea Purée

  1kg frozen petits pois
  20g Ultratex
  100ml extra virgin olive oil

Defrost the peas, then put them into a saucepan of boiling water for 3 minutes. Drain thoroughly, then put the peas into a Vitamix blender with the Ultratex and olive oil and blitz until smooth. Pass through a fine-meshed drum sieve into a bowl and chill over an ice bath. Store in the fridge until needed.

Grilled Baby Onion Petals

  250g silverskin onions
  5g fine sea salt
  Olive oil

Peel the baby onions and cut in half lengthways. Next, make a brine by mixing the fine sea salt with 500ml water. Place the baby onions in a sous-vide bag with the brine and seal under vacuum. Heat a water bath to 85°C and place the bag in it for 15 minutes. Remove the bag from the water and chill in an ice bath. Drain the onions and dry them on kitchen paper. Season with olive oil and salt, then chargrill them in a dry frying pan over a high heat. Separate each petal and trim the root end if necessary.

To Finish

  Blanched peas
  Lettuce spears
  Pea tendrils
  Pink garlic flowers
  Freshly ground mignonette pepper

Prepare and light a Japanese konro grill. Remove the Dexter Beef Short Rib from the sous-vide bag and discard the rendered fat. Grill over charcoal, turning every 5 minutes for about 20 minutes, until warmed through. Put the Pea Purée into a small pan, season with salt and place over a low heat to warm through. Gently reheat the blanched peas and Grilled Baby Onion Petals. Carve the short rib and season with a little salt and mignonette pepper. Swipe 2 spoonfuls of pea purée across each plate, then place the beef across the purée at an angle. Arrange the peas, lettuce, onions, pea tendrils and garlic flowers around the short rib. Reheat the Beef Sauce and add the Smoked Bone Marrow to warm through for 1 minute. Serve the sauce in a jug on the side.

Wild Strawberry Millefeuille, Lemon Verbena, Vanilla, Elderflower

Spring heralds the arrival of the first delicate wild strawberries, as well as the intoxicating elderflower blossoms that complement them so beautifully. Layers of crisp puff pastry protect the delicate fruits, and the generous dots of elderflower, milk and strawberry gels all combine in the mouth to wonderful effect. We choose only the tiniest lemon verbena, Greek basil and sweet cicely leaves to join the delicate elderflowers on top of this very pretty dessert.

Serves 8

Pastry Semicircles

500g Puff Pastry (see page 290)
Flour, for rolling out
100g dextrose powder
100g icing sugar

Preheat the oven to 200°C fan (humidity 30%). Roll out the puff pastry to 4mm thick, then use a 10cm round cutter to stamp out 12 discs. Line a baking tray with baking paper and lay out the pastry discs. Cover with a second piece of baking paper and place a baking tray on top. Bake for 10 minutes. Meanwhile, mix the dextrose and icing sugar together. Remove the discs from the oven and reduce the oven temperature to 180°C no fan. Use a 9cm round cutter to stamp out smaller, neatly edged circles from the baked discs. Dust with the dextrose mixture and return the tray to the oven for 4–6 minutes, until the pastry is glazed and shiny. Allow to cool, then cut the discs in half. Store in an airtight container until needed.

Strawberry Gel

The setting agent agar agar needs to be boiled for two minutes to ensure that it has totally dissolved in the liquid and therefore been activated. Since it has a firmer set than gelatine, we blitz the gel in a blender to break it down and create a more flexible fluid gel for plating.

500g Boiron strawberry purée
50ml Stock Syrup (see page 290)
15g lemon purée
8g agar agar
Fraise des bois liqueur

Put the strawberry purée, stock syrup and lemon purée into a saucepan over a medium heat, whisk in the agar agar and bring to the boil for 2 minutes. Pour into a tray and place in the fridge to set. Once set, transfer the gel to a Vitamix and blend until smooth. Season with a little fraise des bois liqueur, then pass through a fine-meshed drum sieve and store in a squeezy bottle.

Elderflower Gel

520ml elderflower cordial
12g agar agar

Pour the elderflower cordial and 240ml water into a saucepan over a medium heat, whisk in the agar agar and bring to the boil for 2 minutes. Pour into a tray and place in the fridge to set. Once set, transfer the gel to a Vitamix and blend until smooth. Pass through a fine-meshed drum sieve, then store in a squeezy bottle.

Vanilla Milk Gel

900ml whole milk
200ml double cream
150g caster sugar
1 vanilla pod
1g salt
1% Gellan F

Pour the milk and cream into a saucepan and add the sugar, vanilla pod and salt. Place over a medium heat and bring to the boil. Remove from the heat and allow to infuse for 30 minutes. Weigh the liquid to calculate 1% of it, then pour it into a Thermomix. Add the 1% amount of Gellan F and blend at 95°C for 2 minutes. Pour into a tray and place in the fridge to set. Once set, return the gel to the Thermomix and blend at 55°C until smooth. Pass through a fine-meshed drum sieve and store in a squeezy bottle.

Strawberry Jus

We macerate the strawberries in caster sugar to extract as much flavour as possible from the fruit. We then use liquid glucose to finish the sauce because it not only maximises the sweetness and adds viscosity, it is also less likely to crystallise when heated.

1kg fresh strawberries
100g caster sugar
100g glucose
20ml fraise des bois liqueur
5g citric acid

Put the strawberries and sugar into a sous-vide bag with 200ml water and seal under vacuum. Heat a water bath to 85°C and place the bag in it for 2 hours, until the strawberries turn white. Pass through muslin, discarding the solids, and transfer the juice to a saucepan. Add the glucose, then place the pan over a medium–high heat and reduce by half. Add the strawberry liqueur and citric acid to balance the sweetness.

To Finish

Red wild strawberries
Golden wild strawberries
Lemon verbena tips
Sweet cicely tips
Greek basil leaves
White elderflowers
Pink elderflowers

Lay out all the Pastry Semicircles, glazed-side up. On 16 of them, squeeze various-sized dots of all 3 gels and arrange the wild strawberries on their sides. Place half the garnished semicircles on top of the other garnished halves, starting to build the millefeuilles. Finally, place the plain semicircles on top and dot them with the Elderflower Gel and Strawberry Gel. Decorate with the herbs and flowers. Place the millefeuille on a plate and serve the Strawberry Jus in a jug on the side.

Pecan Praline Parfait, Pedro Ximénez, Cocoa Nib Ice Cream

This delicate frozen mousse is a perfect example of how many elements come together to create a beautifully balanced dessert. The creaminess of the silky parfait is offset by the slight bitterness of the cocoa nibs, the salted-caramel pecans and the piquant Pedro Ximénez fluid gel, ensuring that the finished dish is rich but not too sweet to be delicious.

Serves 8

Pecan Praline

250g caster sugar
250g roasted pecans
2g Maldon sea salt

Put the sugar into a saucepan and place over a medium heat until it has dissolved completely and turned a dark golden brown. Add the nuts and swirl the pan to coat them in the caramel. Pour onto a silicone mat and allow to cool completely. When cold, break the praline into shards and put them into a Thermomix. Add the salt and blend until smooth.

Crystallised Cocoa Nibs

100g caster sugar
100g cocoa nibs

Put the sugar into a saucepan with 20ml water and place over a low heat until the sugar has dissolved. Increase the heat and bring to the boil. When the temperature reaches 121°C, pour in the cocoa nibs and stir continuously until they crystallise. Pour onto a silicone mat to cool.

Parfait

The base of this parfait is a pâte à bombe, a type of Italian meringue that uses egg yolks rather than whites. The raw eggs are 'cooked' by adding hot sugar to the mixer as the yolks are whisked, creating a light but rich base for mousses, parfaits and buttercreams. It is important to pour the sugar into the mixer without touching the sides of the bowl or the whisk so that the sugar doesn't crystallise.

50g caster sugar
110g pasteurised egg yolks
350ml double cream
2 gelatine leaves, bloomed in cold water
175g Pecan Praline (see left)
Crystallised Cocoa Nibs (see left)

Put the sugar into a saucepan with 15ml water and place over a low heat until the sugar has dissolved. Increase the heat and bring to the boil. Meanwhile, put the egg yolks into the bowl of a stand mixer and whisk until they have doubled in volume. When the temperature of the sugar reaches 118°C, slowly pour it into the eggs on a low speed, being careful to avoid the sides of the bowl and the whisk. Deglaze the sugar pan with 25ml of the cream, add the bloomed gelatine leaves and place over a low heat to melt. Pour into the egg mixture and continue to mix on a higher speed until cool. This mixture is called a pâte à bombe. In a different stand mixer, whisk the cream to the very soft ribbon stage (semi-whipped). Mix the pecan praline into the pâte à bombe, then fold in the semi-whipped cream. Decant the mixture into a piping bag and pipe into triangular parfait moulds. Cover the top with crystallised cocoa nibs to create the base and place in a blast chiller to freeze.

Cocoa Nib Ice Cream

625ml whole milk
125ml UHT double cream
75g Trimoline
75g caster sugar
25g milk powder
150g cocoa nibs
35g Procrema 100 Cold

Put the milk, cream, Trimoline, sugar and milk powder into a saucepan and bring to the boil. Remove from the heat, pour the hot mixture into a container with the cocoa nibs and allow to infuse for 12 hours. When the time has elapsed, pass the mixture through a fine-meshed sieve, discarding the cocoa nibs, then blend in the Procrema powder using a hand-held blender. Freeze the liquid in Pacojet beakers. For service, churn the ice cream in a Pacojet machine.

Chocolate Brioche Tuile

Toasting the brioche brings out its sweetness and ensures the tuiles have that unmistakable rich brioche flavour. Roughly chop slices of the sweet bread and put them into an oven heated to 100°C for 30–45 minutes, then allow to cool to room temperature before weighing out 250g for this recipe.

250g isomalt
250g glucose
250g dried toasted brioche
40g cocoa powder

Preheat the oven to 170°C no fan. Put the isomalt and glucose into a saucepan and heat to a light caramel. Pour the caramel onto a silicone mat to set. Blitz the brioche to a fine crumb in a Robot Coupe, then mix with the cocoa powder. Once the caramelised sugar has completely cooled, blitz to a fine powder in a Robot Coupe, then add the cocoa brioche and mix together. Sprinkle the mixture thoroughly over a silicone mat placed on a baking tray, then stamp out tuiles using a 7mm round cutter. Bake for 5 minutes, then allow to cool. Store in an airtight container until needed.

Pedro Ximénez Gel

50ml Pedro Ximénez sherry vinegar
250ml Pedro Ximénez sherry
100ml Stock Syrup (see page 290)
8g agar agar

Pour the PX vinegar, sherry and stock syrup into a saucepan over a medium–high heat, whisk in the agar agar and bring to the boil for 1–2 minutes. Pour into a tray and place in the fridge to set for 1 hour. Once set, blitz the gel to a purée with a hand-held blender and pass through a fine-meshed drum sieve to get rid of any lumps. Pour the gel into a squeezy bottle for service.

Candied Pecans

50g pecan halves
50g caster sugar

Preheat the oven to 170ºC fan. Put the nuts
into a small saucepan with the sugar and
75ml water and place over a high heat. Bring
to the boil and cook for 8 minutes. Strain off
any remaining liquid through a fine-meshed
chinois, then spread the nuts over a baking tray
lined with a silicone mat. Place in the oven for
6 minutes, until caramelised. Set aside to cool.
Cut each pecan half into 3 pieces and store
in an airtight container until needed.

Chocolate Spray

250g Valrhona Caramélia chocolate
100g melted cocoa butter

Melt the chocolate and stir through the cocoa
butter. Decant the mixture into a chocolate
spray gun. Remove the parfaits from their
moulds and spray all over with chocolate.
Return the parfaits to the freezer until service.

To Finish

Gold leaf

Remove the Parfaits from the freezer and
place them in the middle of chilled plates.
Decorate the surface of the parfaits with
dots of the Pedro Ximénez Gel, pieces of gold
leaf and Candied Pecans. Place a Chocolate
Brioche Tuille on top of each parfait, followed
by a rocher of the Cocoa Nib Ice Cream.

Summer

As spring turns into summer, fresh produce starts to arrive in a variety of bright colours, offering brilliant flavours and scents that really get the creative juices flowing. There is no better example of this than the pungent, vegetal smell of tomato leaves and vines, which, at its most intense, indicates that the plump red fruits are ready for eating. It is truly evocative of summer.

The chefs in our kitchen, sorry to see the end of spring, are reinvigorated by the wonderful array of produce that starts to flood in from June onwards – everything from artichokes, aubergines, beetroot, courgettes, fennel and mangetout, to cucumber, new potatoes, peas, salad leaves and spring onions. Alongside these are beautiful berries and stone fruits, and an amazing range of herbs and edible flowers that make wonderful garnishes for so many dishes.

Excellent seafood and fish are among the great joys of summer eating. Lobster is at its best, and Cornish crab is simply stunning. We serve it in its carapace with a melon mousse and saffron mayonnaise. Sea bass, too, is an absolute star, cooked with a crisp skin and served with dill pickle, buttermilk dressing and fine herbs.

The arrival of summer changes the mood of everyone in the kitchen, lifting the spirits and bringing a new lightness to the menu. That's because the beautiful produce is fragile, with a short shelf life, so a deft touch is required to bring out its best characteristics. With fruit, for example, we have to ensure it comes at its peak with the right degree of ripeness. We also constantly consider what and how much we need for that day and perhaps one day ahead, and store it carefully to ensure that it reaches our guests in optimum condition. There is no better time to celebrate fruit than summertime, and it can be used in so many creative ways.

Inspirational ingredients

Tomatoes
As tomatoes have a vitally important place in our kitchen, we are very fussy about where and how they are grown. We get heirloom varieties and an array of colours from Isle of Wight growers, but we also have a farmer called Jake, who's based just outside Cambridge and grows a number of things for us, including tomatoes. This is no small undertaking, as we want many different varieties, sizes, colours and flavours. In fine dining it's easy to get caught up in precision, when often what's needed is to let nature do its thing and provide maximum flavour. Tomatoes are a great example of that. Whether tiny or large, rainbow-coloured, striped, pear-shaped, pineapple-flavoured, meaty and seedless, or juicy and full of seeds, tomatoes provide adventures in cooking and eating. Even unripe ones can be used to make a beautiful green tomato and basil vinaigrette that we serve in winter with turbot.

Tomatoes are best stored at room temperature, never in the fridge. Any that are surplus to our needs are peeled and deseeded, covered in olive oil, sprinkled with salt, garlic and thyme and left to macerate for about 20 minutes. They are then transferred to a tray and placed in the oven or a dehydrator overnight to slowly semi-dry and concentrate their beautiful flavour. Meanwhile, dipping bread in the tomato juice left in the bowl is something all our chefs fight over, as it's absolutely delicious.

Tomatoes really come into their own with our blanched lobster tail, which is served with a medley of heirloom tomatoes – some whole, others in slices or wedges, confit or dehydrated – and dressed with a Tahitian vanilla and cherry vinegar vinaigrette.

We also make a tomato dashi (umami broth) by chopping up lots of beautifully ripe tomatoes and blending them with herbs, celery, celery leaves, basil, thyme, a touch of white balsamic vinegar and some salt. We then hang that mixture in a muslin bag over a bowl to extract the tomato water. After that, the water is transferred to a pan, a piece of kombu is added and it's heated until almost boiling. During that time, impurities rise to the surface, so we strain the broth and let it cool. The end result is a pure, clear tomato dashi with a mind-blowing umami flavour that has hints of kombu too. We serve it chilled, in teacups, as an amuse-bouche in summertime, and guests are astonished by its intensity of flavour.

Cumbrian Blue Grey beef
Cumbrian Blue Grey beef comes from a breed that is a cross between Shorthorn and Belted Galloway. It is small-bodied with beautiful intermuscular marbling

that occurs naturally. Although traditionally regarded as a dairy cow, the flavour of its meat is unmatched. The cows are mainly grass-fed, but in the last eight weeks of growth they are given a grain supplement which helps with the marbling. In fact, it's not unlike the marbling found in premium wagyu, and the fat has a sweet nuttiness to it.

We get our supply from Lake District Farmers, a cooperative of about 50 tiny farms that produce small quantities of Cumbrian Blue Grey beef with amazing dedication and attention to detail. The great thing is that we know exactly which farmer has raised the beef we get in; its provenance can be traced literally from paddock to kitchen door.

We work very closely with the cooperative to ensure the specifications we need for the restaurant, discussing how we are going to use it, cook it and turn the farmers' hard work into a dish that puts it on a pedestal. At our request, as an experiment to retain moisture in the beef but develop more flavour, they increased the dry-ageing process from 65 days to 100 days. Together we selected the right sirloins that would be able to do that. We then rendered down some tallow, and the ends of the sirloin on the bone were dipped into it so that the exposed meat was protected by an extra layer of fat. It then went into the Himalayan salt fridge for 100 days.

After that time, we took out the sirloins and broke the tallow away. The flavour and aroma of that beef when it was coming up to room temperature was intoxicating – the sweet smell of umami. We then placed a single steak in a pan without oil, just until the natural fat rendered, and finished cooking it in the oven. The flavour of that beef and the fat was something our team has never forgotten. It was one of the most incredible eating experiences we've had collectively.

Buoyed by the success of this experiment, we then worked with the cooperative to develop key specifications of the sirloin, considering the natural fat content of the animal in order to achieve the best outcome.

While ageing is really important, there's no point in starting with an inferior product and hoping the process will improve it. The key, whether it's produce, a protein or wine, is to start with the best possible product, and the Cumbrian Blue Grey is exactly that. We cook it with the fat on to keep all that flavour in the pan. In the kitchen everyone wants a taste of the rendered, crisp fat cap, a perk we call the chef's snack.

In Restaurant Gordon Ramsay there are times you don't mess with the classics, so in summer we serve the Cumbrian Blue Grey simply as steak and chips. Three pieces of this sirloin, cooked medium rare, are served with baby cosberg lettuce dressed with thickened Japanese vinegar and garnished with pickled shallots, croutons, capers and pink society garlic flowers.

For the 'chips' element, we took inspiration from panisse, a thick batter made from chickpea flour, which is served in the south of France. We cook out the flour with milk and olive oil, and season it with a spice mix normally found on the outside of pastrami. As the mix cooks out, it thickens to the consistency of pomme purée. We pour it into a tray and let it set, then slice it into crinkle-cut chips that are deep-fried.

The finished dish is served with black garlic purée, a red wine beef sauce, pickled mustard seeds and wild garlic capers. It's steak and chips, but delivered with a touch of playfulness and as much attention to detail as everything we do.

Lobsters
Crustacea and shellfish are plentiful in UK waters, but the native lobster is a particular star, endlessly versatile and a wonderful companion to many other flavours. Its shell is gorgeously coloured in shades of blue, and inside is the most delicious meat. Lobsters are available all year round, but are at their best during the summer months. We use relatively small ones, about 500–600g, because this size best suits our purposes, and the meat is beautiful and sweet. There is a common misconception that it should eat like butter, but the tail, which is used for swimming and warding off predators, is well exercised, so has a certain amount of firmness to its texture. We believe that natural texture should be celebrated, so we feature it in a number of our dishes.

In the kitchen we divide the raw lobster into its various parts – tail, legs, claws – and cook them separately because they have different cooking times; we would never cook a whole lobster in a pot of boiling water. In the summertime we simply blanch the flesh, but at other times of year we may grill the blanched lobster over binchotan (Japanese charcoal) to give some smokiness to the sweet flesh, or serve it in lobster ravioli, a signature dish that has been on the menu since Aubergine days. Of course, it has evolved over time, but remains a dish of absolute finesse, being rich, yet light and delicate.

Stone fruits
Peaches, plums, apricots and other stone fruits have many uses in our kitchen. Our supplies tend to come from Spain and southern France, where the climate is perfect for growing them. However, the UK grows some fantastic cherries, and we make good use of them too.

During a recent experiment to use stone fruits differently, we tried out unusual combinations, using the fruit to bring a level of acidity in much the same way as tomatoes or citrus. One of the dishes created was lobster with cherry purée, cherry cheeks and fresh green almonds, finished with a lobster bisque highlighted by cherry juice. It proved to be a lovely combination. In fact, cherries tend to feature heavily on our summer menu. They appear in roast duck with turnip and shiso, and are the hero ingredient in cherry parfait with almond and sweet cicely.

Apricots are fantastic too, going beautifully with fennel and pigeon, but working equally well with cheese. We use heavenly Rove de Garrigues, a goats' cheese from Provence, because it is sweet, nutty and creamy, a world away from some goats' cheeses, which have a distinct barnyard flavour. We accompany it with a slightly sour apricot purée and some dried apricots that we macerate in a little Sauternes. To serve, we crumble the cheese into the purée, add some toasted buckwheat to bring an earthy flavour, then microplane macadamia nuts over the top, and add a dash of elderflower honey to bring it all together.

With stone fruits, it's imperative to consider their ripeness because this will determine what they're used for. We aim for fruit that will take a day or two to ripen. This is particularly true of apricots, which are no sooner ripe than they are heading towards being overripe. Sometimes, however, a dish can benefit from being paired with slightly underripe stone fruit. Our pigeon dish, for example, uses warmed apricots that are just a little underripe, not green and crunchy, to bring a pleasing acidity. The slightly firmer flesh also suits the heating process and gives a better outcome.

If we find ourselves with underripe apricots that have furry-textured flesh, we compress wedges of them in a marinade of Jurançon wine, water and herbs for a few hours before service, and they become intensely flavoured and juicy. This technique allows us to use fruit that would otherwise be unsuitable, so it is beneficial in two ways: excellent flavour and less waste.

Berries
Among the early arrivals in our kitchen are berries, appearing just as spring tips into summer, but the first deliveries come from France because the UK berry season starts later, once the weather has sufficiently warmed up.

Over the course of the summer we receive many amazing varieties of strawberry, but we get most excited about wild ones, sometimes called alpine strawberries. They come from Malaga in Spain, and are possibly the most expensive on the market. These berries have a heady aroma, almost like sweets, but need to be used within five days of picking. It's a small window of opportunity, but one we never miss.

There are, of course, wonderful British strawberries too, which arrive at a similar time to blackberries, blueberries and fantastic Scottish raspberries. The raspberries, which may be red or golden, have a striking flavour that is both sweet and sharp. We use them alongside our decadent chocolate delice, which is partnered with biscuit ice cream, a raspberry gel and a garnish of fresh raspberries.

In summer we always have a berry dessert of some description, and the approach in our kitchen is often about classics, such as strawberries and cream. The key is to get the very best strawberries and allow them to be the hero of the dish, while all the other elements play supporting roles. We often use a strawberry or raspberry liqueur to heighten the flavour of the berries, and add an elderflower vinegar for contrast. The cream element is often a parfait or ice cream.

While berries work really well in desserts, they can also be used to enhance game, such as pigeon, duck and venison. We particularly like to use them with grouse, which is another highlight of the summer. We roast the bird on its crown and serve it with beetroot, pickled blackberries and a single malt whisky gel. In fact, pickling is a great way to preserve the summer bounty of blackberries for future use.

In late summer we use sloe berries, gathered from blackthorn bushes, to make sloe gin, which we offer to guests as a digestif around Christmas time. It's a seasonal favourite that can be used throughout the year.

112 Restaurant Gordon Ramsay

Cornish Crab, Melon, Calamansi, Anise Hyssop

Sweet white crab meat is one of the key flavours of summer in the restaurant. We pair it with ripe Charentais melons from France and more exotic finger limes, originally from Australia. Also known as lime caviar, these citrus fruits are full of juicy, fragrant pearls that literally burst in the mouth. They bring a distinct flavour and welcome acidity to the creamy crab and saffron emulsion, which in turn is balanced beautifully by the sweet melon mousse.

Serves 8

Crab Meat

1 brown crab (2–3kg)
½ carrot
½ leek
½ onion
½ fennel bulb
½ lemon
10g chervil
10g flat-leaf parsley
5g coriander seeds
250ml white wine
250ml white wine vinegar

Place the crab in the freezer for 30 minutes. Peel the vegetables and cut into small dice. Slice the lemon half into 4 pieces and place in a large saucepan with the diced vegetables, herbs and coriander seeds. Add the wine and vinegar and cover with 3 litres of water. Place the pan over a medium–high heat and bring to the boil. Once boiling, add the crab and cook for 8 minutes. Take the pan off the heat and allow the crab to cool in the liquid for 30 minutes. Remove the crab from the pan, along with any legs that may have fallen off during the cooking process. To break down the crab, remove the claws and legs. Next, remove the top shell, exposing the body. Lightly rinse the body and remove the dead man's fingers. Using scissors or the back of a knife, carefully remove the remaining shell from the body, legs and claws, removing as much meat as possible in the process. Set the meat aside and clean away any shell and mess. Spread the meat over a clean plastic tray and carefully pick through it to ensure all the shell has been removed. Keep in the fridge until needed.

Melon Mousse

50ml Stock Syrup (see page 290)
2 gelatine leaves, bloomed in cold water
250ml Charentais melon juice
50g pasteurised egg whites
5ml calamansi vinegar
1g fine sea salt

Pour the stock syrup into a small saucepan and warm over a low heat. Add the gelatine leaves and stir until melted. Put the melon juice, egg whites, vinegar and salt into a bowl and add the stock syrup. Stir and allow to set in the fridge for 2 hours. Once set, beat the mixture with a whisk and place in an espuma gun loaded with 2 nitrous oxide charges. Keep in the fridge.

Calamansi Gel

250g Boiron calamansi purée
100ml Stock Syrup (see page 290)
50ml calamansi vinegar
9g agar agar

Put the calamansi purée, stock syrup, vinegar and 50ml water into a saucepan over a medium–high heat, whisk in the agar agar and bring to the boil for 2 minutes. Pour into a tray and place in the fridge to set for 1 hour. Once set, transfer the gel to a Vitamix and blend until smooth. Pass through a fine-meshed drum sieve, then pour into a squeezy bottle for service.

Saffron Emulsion

An emulsion is a combination of two liquids that don't automatically mix, such as oil and vinegar. Instead, they need to be agitated with a whisk or blender to bind them together. In this case, egg yolks and oil are combined to create the very stable emulsion more familiarly known as mayonnaise.

40g pasteurised egg yolks
20g Dijon mustard
25ml rice wine vinegar
5g fine sea salt
1g saffron powder
5g smoked paprika
2g piment d'Espelette chilli powder
2g freshly ground black pepper
20ml calamansi vinegar
20g slow-roasted garlic (see Parmesan
    Velouté method, page 179)
250ml grapeseed oil

Put all the ingredients, apart from the grapeseed oil, into a Vitamix and blend for 2 minutes on medium speed. Reduce the speed so the mixture is falling back on itself, creating a vortex, and slowly add the oil to emulsify. Transfer to an airtight container and store in the fridge until needed.

To Finish

2 tbsp finely chopped shallots
1 tbsp finger lime flesh (citrus caviar)
3 tbsp chopped dill
Piment d'Espelette chilli powder
Shiso leaves
Anise hyssop leaves
Marigold leaves
Shiso flowers
Coriander flowers
Alyssum flowers
Fine sea salt

Mix 360g of the Crab Meat with the shallots, finger lime flesh and dill, then add a little of the Saffron Emulsion to bind it together. Season with salt. Spoon the crab mixture into 4cm rings inside cleaned crab shells and dot the surface with Calamansi Gel. Using an espuma gun, dispense the Melon Mousse into the ring on top of the crab meat, then remove the ring. The mousse should slowly fall to coat the crab. Sprinkle with a little piment d'Espelette and garnish with the herbs and flowers.

Native Lobster Tail, Tomato, Summer Herbs, Tahitian Vanilla

Lobster is a favourite ingredient in the restaurant, and we serve it all year round with different garnishes, depending on the season. In summer, it is all about tomatoes. We mix fresh heirloom varieties with semi-dried plum tomatoes and datterini 'raisins' for a combination of flavours and textures, then emphasise their sweetness and that of the lobster with a Tahitian vanilla and Pedro Ximénez vinaigrette.

Serves 8

Lobster Preparation

8 × 500g native lobsters
100ml white wine vinegar

Put the lobsters into the freezer for 30 minutes prior to preparing. Bring a large saucepan of water to the boil with the vinegar. Wearing kitchen gloves, separate the tail from the body and remove the claws. Reserve the body and claws for the oil. Pinch the middle fin of the tail and twist carefully, pulling out the entrails; if unsuccessful, use kitchen pliers to remove them. Insert 2 long wooden skewers down the back of the tails so they are straight. Blanch them in the boiling water for 2½ minutes. Lift out of the pan and allow to cool at room temperature for 2 minutes before removing the skewers. Using scissors or the back of a heavy knife, carefully crack the shell to remove it from the tail, reserving the shells for the oil. Trim a little off the body end of the tail to neaten. Place the tails on a tray lined with kitchen paper and store in the fridge until required.

Lobster Oil

Lobster claws and shells, reserved from previous step
2 litres pomace oil, plus extra for frying
1 carrot, peeled and diced
1 onion, peeled and diced
2 celery sticks, diced
1 leek, diced
1 bay leaf
4 thyme sprigs
10 white peppercorns
20 coriander seeds
5 star anise
1 tbsp fennel seeds
1 dried liquorice stick
200g tomato purée
Fine sea salt

Place a large heavy-based saucepan over a high heat, add a little oil and fry the lobster claws and shells until red, caramelised and sweet-smelling. Reduce the heat to medium, add the vegetables, herbs and spices, season with salt and cook for 2 minutes, until aromatic. Stir through the tomato purée and cook for another minute. Add the remaining oil and bring to the boil. Reduce the heat to low and cook very gently for 2 hours, stirring occasionally to make sure it doesn't stick. Strain through a fine-meshed chinois lined with muslin, chill in a bowl placed over an ice bath, then store in an airtight container in the fridge until needed.

Dashi Vinegar Glaze

200ml dashi vinegar
100ml soy sauce
100ml mirin
15g Ultratex

Place all the ingredients in a bowl and whisk together until well combined. Leave for 1 hour so that the Ultratex hydrates, then pass through a fine-meshed drum sieve and set aside until required.

Tahitian Vanilla Vinaigrette

1 Tahitian vanilla pod
50ml Pedro Ximénez sherry vinegar
200ml extra virgin olive oil
5g fine sea salt

Scrape the seeds from the vanilla pod into a bowl and add the sherry vinegar, olive oil and salt. Whisk together to form a vinaigrette, then transfer to a squeezy bottle for service.

Semi-Dried Tomato Petals

6 plum tomatoes
Caster sugar
2 thyme sprigs
1 garlic clove, cracked with the blade of a chef's knife
Extra virgin olive oil

Preheat the oven to 55°C fan. Peel, quarter and deseed the tomatoes, removing the core. Place the petals in a bowl and season with salt and the sugar, then add the thyme and garlic and lightly coat with olive oil. Gently toss the petals and allow to marinate for 20 minutes at room temperature. Transfer to a baking tray lined with baking paper and put them into the oven for 8 hours, until the petals have semi-dried and concentrated their flavour. Place the petals in an airtight container, lightly coat with some more olive oil and store until needed.

Datterini Tomato Raisins

A dehydrator uses heat and circulating air to pull moisture from the centre of fresh fruit and vegetables without removing any of the flavour or nutrients. We semi-dehydrate the datterini tomatoes to make them taste more intense and extra sweet, and to give them a different texture from the fresh tomatoes.

12 yellow datterini tomatoes
12 red datterini tomatoes
250ml tomato juice
2 thyme sprigs
2 garlic cloves, cracked with the blade of a chef's knife
25g caster sugar
Extra virgin olive oil

Peel the tomatoes. Combine the tomato juice, thyme, garlic and sugar in a bowl and season with salt. Add the peeled tomatoes and allow to marinate for 30 minutes. Drain well, then spread them evenly over a tray. Place in a dehydrator heated to 75°C and leave for 2½ hours, until they have shrivelled and shrunk by half. Transfer to an airtight container, dressing them with a little olive oil, and store in the fridge until needed.

To Finish

Selection of heritage tomatoes
Baby ruby basil leaves
Baby marigold leaves
Baby Thai basil leaves
Greek basil leaves
Verbena tips
Chive tips
Green fennel fronds
Bronze fennel fronds
Fennel flowers
Tagete petals
Chive blossoms

Allow the chilled Lobster tails to come up to room temperature, then brush them with the Dashi Vinegar Glaze. Cut the heritage tomatoes into a variety of wedges and slices, depending on their shape. Season the tomatoes with a little salt and dress with the Tahitian Vanilla Vinaigrette. Place a lobster tail in the middle of a plate and arrange the dressed tomatoes, Semi-Dried Tomato Petals and Datterini Tomato Raisins around it. Garnish with all the herbs, fronds and flowers. Finish at the table with a drizzle of Lobster Oil over the dish.

Sea Bass, Dill, Buttermilk, Caviar

There is more to this pretty sea bass dish than meets the eye ... Tiny balls of golden Oscietra caviar lurk under the surface of the stunning buttermilk and dill dressing, waiting to burst in the mouth when eaten. Then the beautiful leaves and flowers conceal dots of punchy dill pickle gel, which brings an unexpected piquancy to the mild, buttery fish and creamy sauce.

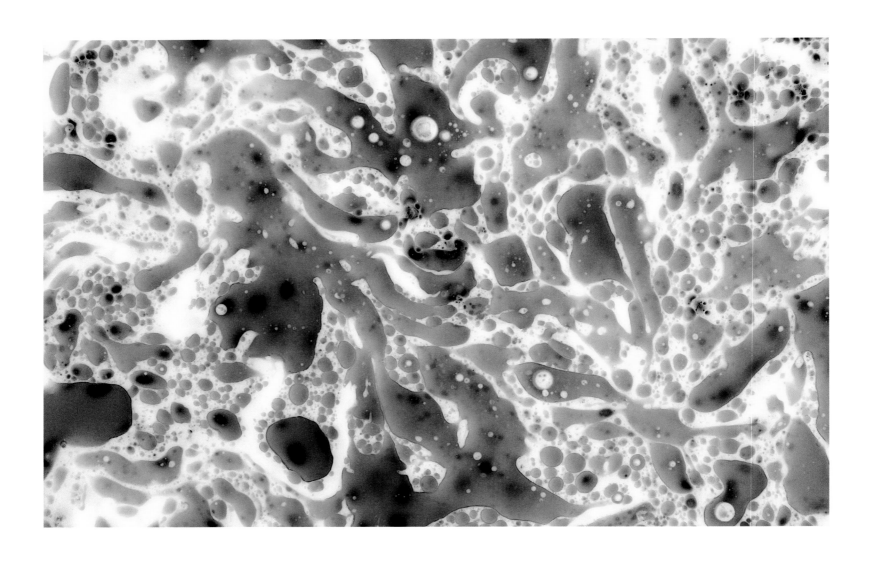

Serves 8

Dill Oil

500g dill, leaves picked
1 litre pomace oil
Fine sea salt

Place the dill and a pinch of salt in a
Thermomix and blend to a fine paste. Add
the oil and heat to 75°C. Blend on a medium
speed for 3 minutes, then pour into a bowl
over an ice bath, stirring until chilled. Wrap
in muslin and strain overnight, collecting the
oil in a bowl. Store in an airtight container
until needed.

Sea Bass

100g fine sea salt
1 × 3kg sea bass, scaled, gutted and filleted

Make a 10% brine by dissolving the salt in
1 litre water. Check the fish for any scales and
remove the pin bones, then place the fillets
in the brine for 10 minutes. Lift out and pat
dry. Allow to air-dry, uncovered, in the fridge
for 24 hours. Cut each fillet into 4 portions
and score the skin 5 times.

Nori Matcha Powder

Nori is a dried seaweed that comes in sheets
that are generally used to wrap around maki
and other rolls in Japanese sushi restaurants.
Toasting nori under the grill reduces its
moisture content, which means that it is
crisp enough to blitz into a powder with the
matcha tea.

10 nori sheets
25g matcha powder

Preheat a grill to high. Put the nori sheets
onto a baking tray and place under the grill
until they start to colour lightly. Set aside
to cool completely. Put the cold nori sheets
into a Vitamix with the matcha and blitz to a
powder. Transfer to an icing duster for service.

Dill Pickle Gel

Usually used for pickling small cucumbers,
we treat dill pickling liquid as an ingredient
in its own right. It is the perfect combination
of sugar, vinegar, garlic, salt and dill to cut
through the creaminess of the fish and the
buttermilk dressing.

500ml dill pickle liquid
10g agar agar

Put the dill pickle liquid into a saucepan over
a medium heat, whisk in the agar agar and
bring to the boil for 2 minutes. Pour into a
tray and place in the fridge to set. Transfer
the gel to a Vitamix and blend until smooth.
Pass through a fine-meshed drum sieve,
then pour into a squeezy bottle for service.

Buttermilk Dressing

300ml whole milk
200ml buttermilk
200g crème fraîche
20ml dashi vinegar
3g fine sea salt

Mix the milk and buttermilk together in
a bowl and add the crème fraîche, dashi
vinegar and salt. Stir to combine, then
transfer to a squeezy bottle for service.

To Finish

Beurre Noisette (see page 289)
Chervil leaves
Small nasturtium leaves
Baby oyster leaves
Anise hyssop leaves
Chive tips
Yarrow tips
Dill fronds
Allium flowers
Alyssum flowers
Golden Oscietra caviar

Warm some beurre noisette in a non-stick pan
over a medium heat and place the Sea Bass
pieces in it, skin-side down. Place a weight on
top and cook until golden brown and the skin
is crisp. Remove the weight, turn the fish over
and cook the flesh side for 15 seconds. Take
off the heat, then dust with the Nori Matcha
Powder. Cover the skin with dots of Dill Pickle
Gel and garnish with the herbs, fronds and
flowers. Pour the Buttermilk Dressing into a
small saucepan and warm gently. Split with the
Dill Oil, then carefully mix through a generous
amount of caviar. Serve this sauce on the side
to be poured around the fish at the table.

Roast Duck, Turnip, Cherry, Shiso

Combining duck and fruit is not new, but serving it with perfectly ripe British cherries at the peak of their season and combining them with the mild bitterness of raw and cooked turnips and aromatic red shiso leaves elevates this dish high above duck à l'orange. The duck itself is topped with crisp sobacha, Japanese roasted buckwheat tea, for a nutty, biscuity flavour and contrasting crunch.

Serves 8

Duck Sauce

1kg duck bones, fat removed and chopped
Vegetable oil
3 shallots, peeled and finely sliced
3 garlic cloves, cracked with the blade
    of a chef's knife
10 white peppercorns
750ml Duke of Sussex Madeira
1 litre Veal Stock (see page 289)
1 litre Chicken Stock (see page 289)
1 thyme sprig
¼ bay leaf
Fine sea salt

Preheat the oven to 200ºC fan. Put the bones into a large roasting tray and season with salt. Roast in the oven for 30 minutes, until golden brown. Place a large, heavy-based saucepan over a medium heat and add a little oil. When hot, add the shallots and garlic and sweat for 2 minutes, until soft. Add the bones and white peppercorns and cover with half of the Madeira. Allow to reduce to a glaze, then add the remaining Madeira and allow to reduce by half. Next, add the stocks, thyme and bay leaf, and bring to the boil, skimming to remove any impurities that may rise to the surface. Simmer until reduced to a sauce consistency. Pass through a fine-meshed sieve lined with muslin and set aside until required.

Cherry Gel

500g Boiron morello cherry purée
50ml Stock Syrup (see page 290)
15ml cherry vinegar
8g agar agar

Put the cherry purée, stock syrup and vinegar into a saucepan over a medium heat, whisk in the agar agar and bring to the boil for 2 minutes. Pour into a tray and place in the fridge to set. When set, transfer the gel to a Vitamix and blend until smooth. Pass through a fine-meshed drum sieve, then pour into a squeezy bottle for service.

Baby Tokyo Turnips

24 baby Tokyo turnips

Carefully trim the root from the turnips. Measure 3cm up the stem and cut off the leaves, reserving them for the garnish. Bring a small saucepan of salted water to the boil and blanch the turnips for 2 minutes. Plunge them into iced water for 2 minutes, then drain on kitchen paper. Keep in the fridge until needed.

Honey Glaze

1kg honey
50ml soy sauce
150ml red wine vinegar
15g fine sea salt
70ml Veal Stock (see page 289)

Put all the ingredients into a saucepan and place over a medium–high heat. Bring to the boil and allow to reduce to a glaze with a consistency similar to honey.

Roast Duck

2 whole dry-aged ducks (2.5kg in total)

Preheat the oven to 200ºC fan. Remove the wings at the second joint and save for the sauce. Turn one of the ducks over, make an incision around the neck, then peel back the skin and remove the neck bone, reserving it for the sauce. Turn the duck back over and remove the wishbone carefully so as not to pierce or tear the skin. Cut a 1-metre length of butcher's twine, then, with the duck neck end facing away from you and the skin tucked under, place the middle of the string over the neck where the wishbone was and draw the string around the bird, under the breast meat towards the legs. Cross the string over and tie it tightly behind the point of the breasts – this should plump up the bird. Next, cross the strings over the legs, wrapping them around each leg twice, and tie the ends together securely. Remove any excess string. Repeat this process with the second duck. Coat both birds generously with the cooled honey glaze and place on a wire rack over a roasting tray. Transfer to the oven and cook for 8 minutes. Reduce the temperature to 180ºC and cook for a further 8 minutes. Set aside to rest for a minimum of 30 minutes.

To Finish

Turnip Ribbons (see page 205)
Vinaigrette (see page 290)
Cherry halves
Dragon mustard leaves
Shiso leaves
Turnip leaves
Shiso blossoms
Sobacha
Thyme leaves
Brassica blossoms
Alyssum flowers
Freshly ground mignonette pepper

Lightly coat the turnip ribbons with the vinaigrette and season with salt and mignonette pepper. Roll them up into cylinders and arrange them on the plate. Gently reheat the Baby Tokyo Turnips, dress with a little vinaigrette and place next to the ribbons. Add dots of Cherry Gel, the cherry halves, dragon mustard, shiso and turnip leaves, and shiso blossoms. Gently reheat the Duck by putting it back in the oven for 2 minutes, then carve the breasts from the crown and brush again with the Honey Glaze. Garnish with the sobacha, thyme leaves, brassica blossoms and alyssum flowers. Slice each breast in half lengthways and place on the plate. Gently reheat the Duck Sauce and serve on the side.

THE MORNING AFTER
THE NIGHT BEFORE

When I woke the day after learning that Restaurant Gordon Ramsay would receive three Michelin stars in the forthcoming guide, I felt like a different person, as though a two-tonne elephant had climbed off my shoulders and shuffled away.

When you put years of energy and focus into something, it's extraordinary how the self-imposed pressure can dissipate instantly by hearing a few longed-for words, in this case, 'three Michelin stars'. All the effort, all the time stressing over every tiny detail, every criticism uttered to bring me down ... they simply rolled off my back.

Everything I ever wanted or thought I needed up to that stage in my life was done. Box ticked. I suddenly had a new base from which to launch into all manner of things. My restless nature meant I was always looking for the next challenge, and *The Michelin Guide* would act as a passport for me to take on the world.

Although pretty hung over after the party we'd had to celebrate, I still got up early. It was a bitterly cold morning, but I put on my running gear and set out to get my head round what had happened. My mind was racing with optimism and I desperately wanted to grab opportunity with both hands: 'Carpe diem – seize the day!'

I told myself that I needed to avoid getting lazy or complacent. The restaurant must step up to an even higher level. If people thought three stars were the end of me pushing, they're hadn't seen anything yet. I was absolutely fizzing with energy and elation.

On the day *The Michelin Guide* came out in 2001, Tana gave me the keys to a blue Ferrari 550 Maranello – a reward for all the years of effort and sacrifice it had taken to obtain three stars. As stunning as the car was, the real prize was printed in that book. The ultimate accolade. And because stars can be taken away as well as awarded, I found I'd become the only three-star chef in London.

As a chef, I never doubted my skills, but I wasn't always sure I could make the restaurant a success. The affirmation from *The Michelin Guide* erased that uncertainty. It gave me the confidence to try new things and to give someone else a go at the helm of the kitchen. That person needed the attitude of a winner, the focus and dedication to move from being a good chef to a great chef, because maintaining three Michelin stars would be one hell of a job. And it would involve the whole team raising its game, proving just how good it could become.

Spotting talent in others and encouraging them to spread their wings is hugely important – any good boss will tell you that. And I've always maintained that planning the succession, deciding who will take the reins when you hand over the baton, is another really vital consideration. How else can you let go and avoid being a source of interference in the kitchen?

I'd reached my goal and had plenty more I wanted to achieve outside the restaurant. I had a team that would carry on my vision, allow it to evolve and maintain the highest standard possible. Now I started thinking about the great chefs who had won three Michelin stars and then took on the world. Alain Ducasse and Joël Robuchon, unwittingly, became my role models.

Back then, Ducasse was the leading light among educators, and running three-star restaurants in three different locations: Paris, Monaco and New York. Robuchon too was replicating everything he'd achieved in Paris around the world, notching up an incredible 32 Michelin stars in his lifetime. I was watching these guys and mapping out how they went global.

I spent the next fortnight analysing them – what they did well, how they grew, when they branched out and, even more importantly, what they didn't do. They went from conducting the orchestra to writing the sheet music and handing it over, something I was now keen to explore. It was a very important transition, not just for me, but for the team too. If I had stayed on the pans, the staff would have been restricted and I'd have had a heart attack. I had to follow the advice I'd always given them: don't get chained, get smart. I wanted them to move up the ranks, learning and eventually playing their own tune.

In moving on to the next stage in my career, the pressure became somewhat different. I needed to show maturity and insight, becoming a role model to those who worked for me, convincing them that taking things to a new level would be rewarding and fulfilling, an opportunity to shine. I discussed this in detail with just three or four of the chefs, those who had the potential to rise to the top, those I entrusted to maintain my vision with the brigade.

Trust is an essential part of running a restaurant. You can't do everything by yourself, so you have to acquire the confidence to delegate and show confidence in others. Communicating these things makes for a personal connection that will keep the vision and goals on track, while allowing your select group of chefs to step up and make their own contribution. This has a waterfall effect on the brigade beneath them, encouraging those individuals to progress in their particular ways while constantly aiming high.

Top chefs always fear that passing the baton to others will dilute the strengths they have built up in their restaurants. This tends to make them a little selfish in their choice of successor, as they want their vision to trickle correctly through the team. But this is only possible once the top chef has the experience to let go. I felt I had reached that point in my life, so I didn't struggle with handing over to someone else who would keep the restaurant inspired and pushing the limits. I thrive on seeing others rise to the occasion because Restaurant Gordon Ramsay has played an important part in their ability to do so. For me, it's one of the most gratifying aspects of being in charge.

Delegation brings new excitement, vigour and focus to the team. Everyone is re-energised, including me. The day after being awarded three stars, I started thinking about who I would appoint to replace me, and wondering how the food would evolve with that new person at the helm.

When selecting the right person to lead my team, there are many attributes and characteristics that I consider vital, and these only become clear by spending enough time with the staff in the kitchen. I can spot a leader in a busy brigade, mostly because it comes so naturally to them. Being a great chef, or even a great waiter, does not necessarily mean you'd make a great manager or restaurateur. They are two very different skill sets. The key to choosing the leaders of my teams is finding those who excel at both.

Spotting those who have an underlying desire to continually learn is a good starting point. Then I look for technical skills, an articulate palate and an openness to new experiences, which are all essential to maintain the standard on the plate. Last, but far from least, I want to see a calm, composed manner that ensures an individual can command respect from the team and get the best out of them. This is something I saw early on with Clare Smyth, and both Clare and I saw it in Matt Abé from a young age. Equally, though, they are the sort of individuals who don't accept second best, and demanding that of the team requires clear communication and an ability to be firm, even blunt. It's not personal. It's perfectionism. Nothing leaves their kitchen unless it is exactly right.

I have seen countless chefs cut corners when they are running behind, so they drop their standards to catch up. The right thing to do is to find time to do things properly. There are always solutions to buy time in a restaurant, and cutting corners is not one of them. In a three-Michelin-star restaurant it is completely unacceptable. What's the point of the exercise if you let laziness creep in? Those who have led my team have never succumbed to the urge to let something go to the dining room that isn't quite right.

Being a chef of the highest standard is one thing, but not everyone can be a leader. Some people excel under leaders, but only a few thrive at the top and give space to those below them to grow. Leaders instinctively educate, nurture and empower staff lower down the ladder. And, of course, I'm not there all the time, so I rely on my chef patron to know who has it in them to take over when they leave. For Clare it was Matt, for Matt it is Kim Ratcharoen. All have shown the maturity, skill and nous to make it at three-star level.

In 25 years, I'm pleased to say that I always seem to have made the right choices in spotting and nurturing talent. They have repaid me with hard work and loyalty, which I've done my best to reciprocate. I have ensured they become financially secure, have the freedom to grow, get out of the kitchen regularly so they can touch and taste new produce at its source, sample new restaurants and get inspired about the next step forward. Alongside this, I ensure they come to understand a profit and loss statement and the many other aspects of running a successful restaurant. My aim is to give them everything they need to become a huge success because this reaps dividends for both them and me.

As I planned for the future, I knew I wanted to avoid the mistakes I'd made in my own career. Marco had given me such a generous start, putting me in charge of Aubergine, but I got a bit possessive of it, which led to some big clashes between us. He held me back because he didn't want to let me go, which was flattering, but frustrating. As a direct result of this experience, I behave very differently with the head chefs I appoint. First, I have to recognise that they are leading the kitchen. They can't lead if I'm pulling the strings from above. I have to let go and give them responsibility for making the big decisions. I'm always there as a sounding board, but they need a sense of ownership, of truly making the call on everything from dish creation to structuring the team. No one excels when they are on a leash. Showing trust in them, giving them the freedom to become the best version of themselves, allows them to thrive, and everyone benefits. I want them to get big, and to take on the world for themselves so they can create their own magic.

I have long believed that the restaurant should teach our chefs not simply how to cook, but how to taste. That might sound absurd, but if you don't know how something should taste at its absolute best, then you shouldn't be cooking it. I make a point of getting my chefs to close their eyes and identify the flavours on a plate. If they don't get them 100 per cent right, they shouldn't be cooking that dish. How can you cook something to perfection if you don't know what that perfect moment should taste like?

The ability to pinpoint flavours and get the balance spot on is really important because it stops you going too far with any technique during the cooking process. We teach our chefs to understand that, we empower them to make the right decisions, and we guide them to become the best they can be. The restaurant is, in effect, a little academy that creates alumni who go on to great things.

I had always thought the accolade of three Michelin stars was about me and making my mark, but it was actually far more than that. It was about everyone in the team, and the opportunity it presented to all of them. It was the trigger for opening restaurants thick and fast all over the world, but Restaurant Gordon Ramsay in Chelsea remains the pinnacle, the mothership of excellence in my craft.

Grouse, Beetroot, Pickled Blackberries, Single Malt Whisky

The Glorious Twelfth, otherwise known as the beginning of the grouse season, coincides with the burgeoning of British hedgerows, so the moment we get the first game birds through the door, we are also inundated with gorgeous, ripe blackberries. Together with sweet summer beetroot and the red leaves of purple oxalis and amaranth, they create a sensational garnish. The sweet steam bun hides a filling of confit grouse leg flavoured with cranberry vinegar and single malt whisky.

Serves 8

Grouse Preparation

4 whole grouse

Using a cleaver or similar knife, remove the grouse wings at the second joint, reserving them for the sauce. Next, cut off and discard the head, leaving the neck as long as possible. Roll the grouse over so the breasts are facing down and make an incision along the middle of the neck to split the skin from it. Carefully expose the neck and the crop, being careful not to tear the skin. Now cut off the neck bone and crop as close to the breasts as possible, reserving the neck bone for the sauce. Turn the bird back over and tuck the neck skin underneath, then use a blowtorch to remove any small feathers. Remove the legs and set them aside for the confit process. Make a small cut behind the high point of the breasts, then separate the guts from the crown. Remove and discard all the innards. Thoroughly clean the inside of the crown with kitchen paper. Keep in the fridge until needed.

Confit Grouse Legs

8 grouse legs
100g fine sea salt
1 thyme sprig
1 garlic clove, cracked with the blade
    of a chef's knife
50g duck fat

Using scissors, cut the feet off the grouse legs, then remove the shin parts, reserving them for the sauce. Toss the thighs in the salt until well covered and chill for 1 hour. Rinse thoroughly and pat dry. Place the thighs flat and spaced apart in a sous-vide bag, add the thyme, garlic and duck fat and seal under vacuum. Heat a water bath to 95ºC and place the bag in it for 4 hours. Transfer the bag to an ice bath. Once cool, remove the thigh bones and skin, then gently shred the meat and reserve for later.

Confit Duck Legs

2 duck legs
100g fine sea salt
400g duck fat
2 thyme sprigs
1 bay leaf
2 garlic cloves, cracked with the blade
    of a chef's knife

Generously coat the duck legs in salt and chill for 4 hours. Preheat the oven to 95ºC. Thoroughly wash the salt off the legs and pat dry with kitchen paper. Put the duck fat in a saucepan with the legs, thyme, bay leaf and garlic. Place over a medium heat until the fat has melted. Cover the fat with a cartouche and place a lid on top. Transfer to the oven and cook for 6 hours, until the meat falls easily away from the bone. Remove from the oven, take the lid off the pan and allow to cool at room temperature for 1 hour. Remove the legs from the pan and pull off the meat, discarding the bones, skin and excess fat. Keep the meat in the fridge until needed.

Grouse Sauce

Vegetable oil
1kg chicken wings, roughly chopped
Reserved grouse bones, cleaned and
    roughly chopped
2 shallots, peeled and roughly chopped
2 garlic cloves, cracked with the blade
    of a chef's knife
2 thyme sprigs
10 black peppercorns
20ml cranberry vinegar
50ml crème de mûre liqueur
100ml single malt whisky
1 litre Chicken Stock (see page 289)
1 litre Veal Stock (see page 289)
Fine sea salt

Place a heavy-based saucepan over a medium–high heat, add a little oil and brown the chicken wings and grouse bones until golden and evenly caramelised. Add the shallots, garlic, thyme and peppercorns, season with salt and sweat for 2 minutes. Deglaze the pan with the cranberry vinegar, then add the crème de mûre and whisky and allow to reduce by half. Pour in the stocks and bring to the boil, skimming off any impurities that may rise to the surface. Lower the heat and allow to reduce to a sauce consistency. Pass through a fine-meshed sieve and adjust the seasoning if necessary.

Whisky Gel

400ml single malt whisky
200g Stock Syrup (see page 290)
14g agar agar

Pour the whisky, stock syrup and 100ml water into a saucepan over a medium heat, whisk in the agar agar and bring to the boil for 2 minutes. Pour into a tray and place in the fridge to set. Once set, transfer the gel to a Vitamix and blend until smooth. Pass through a fine-meshed drum sieve, then pour into a squeezy bottle for service.

Beetroot Purée

Pomace oil
4 shallots, peeled and sliced
5 black peppercorns
½ bay leaf
2 thyme sprigs
1 garlic clove, cracked with the blade
    of a chef's knife
1 litre beetroot juice
10g Gellan F
50ml cranberry vinegar

Place a large, heavy-based frying pan over a medium–high heat and add a little oil. When hot, add the shallots and sweat for 2 minutes, until soft but without colour. Season with a pinch of salt, then add the peppercorns, bay leaf, thyme and garlic and continue to cook until the shallots are translucent. Pour in the beetroot juice and bring to the boil. Once boiling, remove from the heat and allow to infuse for 20 minutes. When the time has elapsed, pass through a fine-meshed sieve and transfer the infused juice to a Thermomix. Bring the temperature of the beetroot juice up to 90ºC, then slowly add the Gellan F and blitz at full speed for 2 minutes. Pour into a tray and place in the fridge to set. Once set, blitz in the Thermomix again, but without heat, until it is silky smooth. Season with salt and cranberry vinegar, then pass through a fine-meshed chinois and transfer to a squeezy bottle for service.

Beetroot Ribbons

1 large beetroot
250ml beetroot juice

Cover a chopping board with baking paper to prevent staining and use gloves to protect your hands. Peel the beetroot, then use a vegetable sheeter to cut long beetroot ribbons. Trim the ribbons into strips that are 24cm long and 3cm wide. Put the ribbons and beetroot juice into a lidded container and store in the fridge.

Pickled Blackberries

100g wild blackberries
25ml cranberry vinegar
25ml Stock Syrup (see page 290)

Combine all the ingredients in a sous-vide bag and seal under vacuum. Heat a water bath to 50°C and place the bag in it for 2 hours. Chill in an ice bath and set aside until needed.

Red Wine and Shallot Jam

30ml pomace oil
10 large shallots, peeled and finely sliced lengthways
750ml red wine
375ml ruby port
10g mignonette pepper
20ml cabernet sauvignon vinegar

Place a large, heavy-based saucepan over a medium heat and add the oil. When hot, add the shallots with a pinch of salt and allow to sweat until thoroughly cooked but without colour. Increase the heat, then add the wine and port, bring to the boil and allow to reduce, until the shallots are nicely glazed and sticky. Set aside to cool. Season with the mignonette pepper and vinegar, and more salt if necessary. Store in a lidded container until needed.

Grouse Bun Dough

Dried yeast needs to be activated to do its job of raising the dough. To achieve this, it must be heated to between 37°C and 43°C. If it's too cold, it won't activate, and if it's too hot, the active raising agents will be killed off. We settle on 40°C, in the middle of this range, to make sure it works every time.

120g kirin special soft flour
8g caster sugar
4g milk powder
4g fine sea salt
1g baking powder
1g bicarbonate of soda
4g dried yeast
10g clarified butter

Put the flour, sugar, milk powder, salt, baking powder and bicarbonate of soda into the bowl of a stand mixer and mix together by hand. Place 70ml water in a small saucepan over a low heat. When the water reaches 40°C, add the yeast and clarified butter and stir until incorporated. Pour this into the dry ingredients, mix together with the dough hook, and knead for 10 minutes. Cover with cling film and leave to prove in a warm place for about 1 hour, until the dough has doubled in volume.

Grouse Bun Filling

100ml Grouse Sauce reduction (200ml grouse sauce, see opposite, reduced by half)
1 gelatine leaf, bloomed in cold water
10g finely diced carrot
10g finely diced celeriac
10g finely diced shallot
50g Confit Duck Leg meat (see opposite), finely chopped
50g Confit Grouse Leg meat (see opposite), finely chopped
5g chopped chives
5g chopped chervil
15ml cranberry vinegar
15ml single malt whisky
Freshly ground black pepper

Gently warm the reduced grouse sauce, add the gelatine and stir until melted. Mix the remaining ingredients together, then fold through the sauce. Season with salt and pepper to taste. Allow to cool, then form into 10g balls and chill until needed.

Assembling the Grouse Buns

Preheat a steam oven to 80°C. Divide the dough into 20g balls and use a rolling pin to lightly roll each ball into a 6cm circle. Place a ball of the grouse filling in the centre of each circle and wrap the dough around it, making sure that all the ends are tucked in. Place the buns in a perforated steamer tray, spacing them well apart. Tightly wrap the tray with cling film, then leave the buns to prove for 20 minutes, until doubled in size again. Once proved, remove the cling film and place the tray in the oven for 4 minutes. When the time has elapsed, switch the oven off and open the door, but allow the buns to rest inside for 4 minutes. Cool in the fridge until needed.

Toasted Oat Groats

75g unsalted butter
100g oat groats
2g grated nutmeg
2g freshly ground black pepper

Put the butter into a small saucepan and melt over a medium heat. Add the oats and cook for 5 minutes, stirring regularly, until golden brown. Season with salt, nutmeg and pepper, then strain the oats through a fine-meshed chinois. Spread over a tray lined with kitchen paper to absorb any excess butter. Transfer to an airtight container until required.

Cooking the Grouse Crowns

1 litre Chicken Stock (see page 289)
60g fine sea salt
4 grouse crowns, reserved from first step
Vegetable oil
Unsalted butter, for basting

Put the chicken stock into a high-sided container with 1 litre water and add the salt. Attach a sous-vide circulator to the container and heat to 65°C. Once up to temperature, add the grouse crowns and poach for 12 minutes. Dry the grouse thoroughly with kitchen paper. Place a heavy-based frying pan over a high heat. When hot, add a little oil, then add the grouse and cook for 2 minutes on each side, until golden brown. Add a knob of butter to the pan and baste the birds continually for a further minute. Remove from the pan and allow to rest for 10 minutes.

To Finish

Olive oil
Red amaranth leaves
Purple oxalis leaves
Sweet cicely leaves
Chopped chives
Chive flowers
Heather sprigs, for presentation
Honey Glaze (see page 127)
Puffed amaranth

Preheat a deep-fat fryer to 180°C. Deep-fry the steamed Grouse Buns until they are golden brown all over, then transfer them to a tray lined with kitchen paper and keep warm. Reheat the Red Wine and Shallot Jam and place 2 small quenelles on a plate at an angle next to each other. Remove the Beetroot Ribbons from the beetroot juice, glaze them with a little olive oil and season with salt and mignonette pepper, then gently warm them under a salamander until they soften slightly. Drape the ribbons over the shallot jam, then place dots of Beetroot Purée over and around the ribbons. Next, add the Pickled Blackberries and garnish with the amaranth and oxalis leaves. Top the buns with some Whisky Gel and dip them in the Toasted Oat Groats, then garnish with the sweet cicely, chopped chives and chive flowers. Place the buns in presentation bowls lined with heather. Carve the breasts from the Grouse Crowns and remove the skin, checking for any shot that may still be in the bird. Brush the breasts with honey glaze and coat with toasted oat grouts and puffed amaranth. Place on the plate next to the garnish. Gently reheat the Grouse Sauce and serve on the side.

Herdwick Lamb, Courgette, Romesco, Black Olive

Inspired by a traditional Provençal ratatouille, we serve simply cooked loins
of incomparable Herdwick lamb with a tomato and red pepper romesco sauce,
courgette purée and kalamata olives for a true taste of summer. A hand-made
lamb and black olive sausage sits by a large dot of silky white gel made from
the distinctive Fleur du Maquis ewes' cheese from the island of Corsica.
This is garnished with French piment d'Espelette, a gentle smoky chilli powder
from the Basque region.

Lamb Sauce

500g lamb bones
Vegetable oil
1kg lamb trimmings
2 carrots
2 celery sticks
1 onion
¼ celeriac
1 leek, white part only
2 turnips
10 white peppercorns
1 rosemary sprig
1 thyme sprig
1 bay leaf
2 garlic cloves, cracked with the blade
    of a chef's knife
1 litre Veal Stock (see page 289)
1 litre Chicken Sock (see page 289)
25g marjoram, leaves picked
Barolo vinegar
Fine sea salt

Preheat the oven to 180°C fan. Put the bones
into a roasting tray with a little oil and place
in the oven for 30 minutes, until well browned.
Place a large, heavy-based saucepan over a
high heat, add a little oil and brown the lamb
trimmings all over. Peel the vegetables and
roughly chop into 2cm dice. Add them to the
browned trimmings, season with salt and
sweat for 5 minutes, until tender. Add the
peppercorns, rosemary, thyme, bay leaf and
garlic, then add the roasted bones and the
stocks. Bring to the boil, skimming the surface
regularly. Reduce the heat and allow to simmer
for 45–60 minutes, until a sauce consistency
is achieved. Remove from the heat and add
the marjoram. Allow to infuse for 5 minutes,
then add a splash of Barolo vinegar to taste
and adjust the seasoning if necessary. Strain
through a fine chinois lined with muslin, then
cool and set aside until needed.

Courgette Purée

1kg courgettes
Pomace oil
20g basil, leaves picked
20g verbena, leaves picked
20ml Columbino extra virgin olive oil

Quarter, deseed and finely slice the
courgettes. Place a large sauté pan over
a medium–high heat and, when hot, add
a drizzle of pomace oil. Add the courgettes,
season with salt and sweat with a lid on for
3 minutes. Add the basil and verbena and
cook with the lid off for 2 minutes – there
should be no moisture in the pan. Once tender,
transfer to a Vitamix and blend until smooth.
Add the olive oil and season with salt, then
pass through a fine-meshed drum sieve and
chill in a bowl over an ice bath.

Romesco

50g unsalted butter
100g almonds
100g hazelnuts
5 red peppers
3 plum tomatoes
Vegetable oil
2 shallots, peeled and finely diced
5g piment d'Espelette chilli powder
Bouquet garni (bay leaf, thyme, basil,
    garlic clove in a bouquet garni bag)
1 tbsp tomato purée
200ml tomato juice
Sherry vinegar
Extra virgin olive oil

Place a pan over a medium heat, then add the butter and nuts and constantly move the pan until roasted. Strain through a fine-meshed chinois, discarding the butter, then leave to dry on kitchen paper. Using a blowtorch, char the red peppers until blackened, then scrub to peel off the skin. Finely dice the flesh, discarding the seeds and white pith. Peel, deseed and dice the tomatoes. Heat a little oil in a saucepan over a medium heat and add the shallots. Sweat for 3 minutes, until soft, then add the peppers, tomatoes, piment d'Espelette and bouquet garni, season with salt and cook for 2 minutes. Add the tomato purée and cook for another 2 minutes, then add the tomato juice. Cover with a cartouche, reduce the heat and cook slowly for 30 minutes, until the sauce has thickened. Blitz the nuts in a Robot Coupe until coarsely chopped, then add to the cooked tomato mixture and stir to combine. Taste and adjust the seasoning with salt, sherry vinegar and extra virgin olive oil. Transfer to a covered container and store in the fridge.

Ewes' Cheese Gel

5g sliced garlic
5g sliced shallot
30ml olive oil
500ml whole milk
2g picked marjoram leaves
1g whole white peppercorns
10g fine sea salt
135g Fleur du Maquis cheese, rind removed
8g Gellan F

Put the garlic and shallot into a saucepan and cover with the oil. Place over a low heat and allow to infuse for 5 minutes. Add the milk, increase the heat to medium and bring to the boil. Remove from the heat and add the marjoram, peppercorns and salt. Leave to infuse for 15 minutes. Pass through a fine-meshed chinois and transfer the liquid to a Thermomix, then add the cheese and Gellan F. Blitz until the temperature reaches 90°C, then pour into a tray and place in the fridge to set. Once set, return to the Thermomix and blend until smooth, then pass through a fine-meshed drum sieve. Transfer to a squeezy bottle and keep warm for service.

Dried Black Olive Crumb

200g pitted Kalamata olives
20ml aged balsamic vinegar

Wash the olives under cold running water to remove the excess brine, then allow to drain well. Place the olives and balsamic vinegar in a bowl and mix together. Transfer to a tray, place in a dehydrator heated to 75°C and leave for 24 hours. After the time has elapsed, set the olives aside to cool to room temperature. Use a sharp knife to chop the dried olives to a crumb consistency.

Lamb Sausages

500g minced lamb
200g lamb fat, minced
3g cracked black pepper
3g wild garlic powder
10g fine sea salt
15ml oak-smoked water
15ml brandy
5g marjoram leaves, chopped
15g basil leaves, chiffonade
20g mint leaves, chiffonade
5g freeze-dried tomato powder
10g Dried Black Olive Crumb (see above)
1 × 1m lamb casing
Milk, for soaking

Mix all the ingredients together by hand. Fry a small amount to test the seasoning, and adjust if necessary. Untangle the casing, then rinse it in cold water to wash off the salt. Soak the casing in milk for 5–10 minutes, and rinse again. Using a squeezy bottle, pour oil into the casing to lubricate the inside before filling with the meat mixture. When forming your sausages, make sure there are no air bubbles. Leave the sausages to hang and air-dry in the fridge, preferably overnight.

Lamb Loins

2 Herdwick lamb loins (short saddle)
Vegetable oil

Remove the bark (paper-like layer that covers the fat) from the lamb loin and score the fat in a criss-cross pattern. Remove any sinew from the meat and leave at room temperature for 30 minutes before cooking. Preheat the oven to 180°C fan. Season the loin with salt and place in a warm cast-iron frying pan, fat-side down, over a medium heat. Once the fat has rendered and coloured, sear the sides and back of the loin. Transfer to a wire rack, fat-side up, over a baking tray. Place in the oven for 4 minutes, then turn over and cook for a further 4 minutes. Allow to rest for 10 minutes before carving each loin into 4 pieces.

To Finish

Vegetable oil, for frying
Kalamata olive cheeks
Anise hyssop leaves
Green basil cress
Red basil cress
Marjoram tips
Basil flowers
Marjoram flowers
Fennel fronds
Piment d'Espelette chilli powder

Heat a little oil in a frying pan over a medium heat and cook the Lamb Sausages, turning regularly. Allow to rest for 2 minutes. Gently warm the Courgette Purée and place a large swipe on a plate. Reheat the Romesco and place a quenelle of it on the plate. Garnish with 3 olive cheeks and the herbs, flowers and fronds. Place a large dot of Ewes' Cheese Gel on the plate and sprinkle with a little piment d'Espelette. Place a sausage next to the gel, leaving room to place a piece of Lamb Loin in between. Warm the Lamb Sauce and serve on the side.

100-Day-Aged Cumbrian Blue Grey Beef, Panisse, Cosberg, Black Garlic

Blue Grey is a rare breed of cattle from the north of England, which is renowned for its slow-grown, succulent beef. We choose cuts that have been aged for a hundred days because the flavour and tenderness are second to none, then we serve them with charred cosberg lettuce, panisse chips and black garlic ketchup. It's steak and chips taken to a whole new level.

Serves 8

Wild Garlic Capers

300g wild garlic seed pods
150g coarse sea salt
200ml champagne vinegar

Use a fork to remove the individual garlic seed pods from the stems, then wash them thoroughly under cold running water. Allow them to dry on kitchen paper, then transfer to a small Kilner jar and cover with the salt. Shake together, making sure the salt is evenly distributed, then place in the fridge for 3 weeks. Once the time has elapsed, pour the pods into a fine-meshed chinois and wash under cold running water for 10 minutes, removing all the salt. Transfer to a small, sterilised preserve jar and cover with the vinegar. Seal and chill for a minimum of 1 week.

Black Garlic Purée

300g peeled black garlic
120ml Stock Syrup (see page 290)
120ml champagne vinegar
Fine sea salt

Put the garlic, stock syrup, vinegar and 100ml water into a Vitamix and blend until silky and smooth. Season with salt, then pass through a fine-meshed drum sieve and pour into a squeezy bottle for service.

Beef Sauce

100ml vegetable oil
1.5kg beef trimmings
3 shallots, peeled and sliced
3 garlic cloves, cracked with the blade
    of a chef's knife
10 black peppercorns
1 thyme sprig
½ bay leaf
50ml cabernet sauvignon vinegar
350ml brandy
750ml red wine
1 litre Veal Stock (see page 289)
1 litre Chicken Stock (see page 289)

Place a large heavy-based saucepan over a medium–high heat and add the oil. When hot, add the beef trimmings and cook until browned all over. Add the shallots, garlic and peppercorns and continue to cook for 2 minutes. Next, add the thyme and bay leaf, then deglaze the pan with the vinegar, add the brandy and reduce to a glaze. Pour in the red wine and reduce to a glaze again. Now add the stocks and bring to the boil. Reduce the heat and simmer for 1 hour, removing any scum from the surface and keeping the inside of the pan brushed down. Once cooked, pass through a fine-meshed chinois lined with muslin. Adjust the seasoning, if necessary, then cool and put to one side until needed.

Pickled Mustard Seeds

100g yellow mustard seeds
200ml champagne vinegar
50ml chardonnay vinegar
10g fine sea salt
40g caster sugar

Bring a saucepan of unsalted water to the boil and blanch the mustard seeds for 1 minute. Refresh in cold running water and wash for 5 minutes. Put the vinegars into a saucepan with the salt and sugar and bring to the boil. Remove this pickling liquor from the heat and pour over the mustard seeds. Allow to cool, then store in the fridge until needed.

Pastrami Spice Mix

20g black peppercorns
10g coriander seeds
5g yellow mustard seeds
5g fennel seeds
1g cloves
5g juniper berries
1g ground cinnamon
1g piment d'Espelette chilli powder
1 dried bay leaf

Toast the whole spices in a dry frying pan over a medium heat until aromatic. Allow to cool, then place in a Vitamix with the ground cinnamon, piment d'Espelette and bay leaf and blend to a fine powder. Store in an airtight container.

Panisse Chips

These 'chips' are made with chickpea flour rather than potato, which makes them extremely light and fluffy. Using a batter also means it is possible to fold through flavourings, in this case the pastrami spice mix and freeze-dried tomato powder, which add colour as well as a slight tanginess.

850ml whole milk
235g gram flour
50ml olive oil
50g unsalted butter
25g fine sea salt
10g freeze-dried tomato powder
3g Pastrami Spice Mix (see above)

Put all the ingredients into a Thermomix and blend for 15 minutes at 85°C. Spread over a tray lined with baking paper, cover with cling film and put into the fridge to cool. Once cold, cut into crinkle-cut chip shapes with a crinkle-cut knife, and store on kitchen paper in the fridge until needed for cooking.

Croutons

2 slices pain de mie, 1cm thick
50g clarified butter
1 thyme sprig
1 garlic clove, cracked with the blade
    of a chef's knife

Remove the crusts from the bread, then use a rolling pin to gently compress each slice so that it is 5mm thick and easier to cut into regular 5 × 5mm cubes. Place a frying pan over a medium heat and add the clarified butter, thyme and garlic. Once aromatic, add the diced bread, season with salt and fry the croutons until they are golden brown all over. Strain off the butter and allow the croutons to cool on kitchen paper to absorb any excess butter. Once cooled, store in an airtight container until needed.

Pickled Shallot Rings

4 banana shallots, peeled
200ml House Pickling Liquor (see page 289)

Using a mandoline, slice the shallots into circles 3mm thick. Separate the rings, discarding any that are damaged or not round. Bring the house pickling liquor to the boil in a small pan. Pour it over the shallot rings and season with salt. Leave to cool at room temperature, then place everything in an airtight container and store in the fridge until required.

100-Day-Aged Cumbrian Blue Grey Beef

The steaks are turned regularly as they are cooked over a high heat to ensure they build up a really good crust on the outside, but without allowing the internal heat to rise too high, as this would result in an overcooked piece of meat.

3 sirloin steaks, each 8cm thick

Preheat the oven to 200°C fan. Place a large, cast-iron frying pan over a medium heat. Generously season one of the steaks with salt. Put the steak into the dry, warm pan fat-side down and cook gently until the fat has rendered and caramelised. Remove the steak from the pan and turn the heat up to high. When the fat is smoking, return the steak to the pan and continue to colour the remaining sides, turning frequently from side to side until golden brown all over. Remove from the pan and place on a roasting rack over a baking tray. Repeat this process with the remaining steaks. Once all the steaks have been seared, put the tray into the oven for 4 minutes. Turn the steaks over and cook for a further 4 minutes. Remove from the tray and allow to rest for 10 minutes.

To Finish

Dashi Vinegar Glaze (see page 119)
4 cosberg lettuce hearts, halved
Society garlic flowers
Chive tips
Chervil tips
Allium buds
Amaranth leaves
Chopped chives
Finely diced shallots
Flaky sea salt and freshly ground
    mignonette pepper

Preheat a deep-fat fryer to 170°C. Deep-fry the Panisse Chips until they are golden brown. Drain on kitchen paper, then place on a side plate with a liberal amount of Black Garlic Purée. Generously brush the cut side of each lettuce half with the dashi vinegar glaze. Arrange the Pickled Shallot Rings, Wild Garlic Capers, Croutons, flowers, herb tips, buds and leaves on top, then transfer the lettuce hearts to larger plates. Carve the Cumbrian Blue Grey Beef into thick slices and season with a little flaky sea salt and mignonette pepper. Gently warm the Beef Sauce and finish with the chopped chives, shallot brunoise and Pickled Mustard Seeds. Serve on the side to be poured at the table.

Rove de Garrigues, Apricot, Elderflower Honey, Macadamia Nut

Rove de Garrigues is a fresh, rindless cheese from the Pyrenees mountains in France. It is made from the milk of goats that are allowed to roam freely through the woods and arid grasslands of the area, so the cheese carries the flavours of the chestnuts and herbs that they eat, depending on the season. In summer, it tastes sharp and lemony, with floral notes and a hint of thyme, which makes it a beautiful partner for apricots, elderflowers and honey.

Serves 8

Marinated Apricots

100g dried apricots
50ml Sauternes

Cut the apricots into quarters and put them into a bowl. Cover with the wine and place in the fridge to marinate for 24 hours.

Apricot Gel

500g Boiron apricot purée
15ml apricot liqueur
30ml chardonnay vinegar
6g agar agar

Place the apricot purée, liqueur and vinegar in a small saucepan over a medium heat, whisk in the agar agar and bring to the boil for 2 minutes. Pour into a tray and place in the fridge to set. Once set, transfer the gel to a Vitamix and blend until smooth. Pass through a fine-meshed drum sieve, then pour into a squeezy bottle for service.

Elderflower Honey

50g fresh elderflower heads
225g blossom honey
10ml chardonnay vinegar

Put the elderflower heads into a sous-vide bag with the honey and vinegar and seal under vacuum. Heat a water bath to 75°C, add the bag and leave for 15 minutes. Remove the bag and allow to cool at room temperature for 2 hours. Strain the honey through a fine-meshed chinois into an airtight container and store in the fridge until required.

To Finish

4 × 80g Rove de Garrigues cheeses
Macadamia nuts
Sobacha
Bee pollen

Crumble each cheese into 10 pieces, placing 5 pieces in each bowl. Add 5 pieces of the Marinated Apricots and 6 dots of Apricot Gel in and around the cheese. Microplane 2 macadamia nuts over the top of each bowl, then sprinkle over the sobacha and bee pollen. Drizzle with Elderflower Honey to finish.

Cherry Parfait, Almond, Sweet Cicely, Oxalis

A beautifully pink cherry mousse hides within this perfect white-chocolate shell. Flavoured with hibiscus and the juice of two different types of cherry, it is wonderfully light and fragrant, with a crunchy base of toasted almonds. The parfait is served with a supporting cast of fresh cherries, green almonds and the delicate leaves of sweet cicely, purple oxalis and amaranth.

Serves 8

Cherry Reduction

1kg Boiron morello cherry purée
100g amarena cherries
20ml cherry syrup
40g dried hibiscus flowers

Put the morello cherry purée into a saucepan with the amarena cherries, the cherry syrup and hisbiscus. Place the pan over a medium heat, bring to the boil and allow to reduce by half, stirring occasionally to make sure it doesn't catch. Allow to cool at room temperature for 30 minutes. Transfer to a Vitamix and blend until smooth, then store until required.

Cherry Parfait

700ml double cream
100g caster sugar
225g pasteurised egg yolks
400ml Cherry Reduction (see above)
4 gelatine leaves, bloomed in cold water
100g nibbed almonds, toasted

Put 600ml of the cream into the bowl of a stand mixer and whisk to soft ribbons. Next, put the sugar into a saucepan with 15ml water and place over a low heat until the sugar has dissolved. Increase the heat and bring to the boil. Meanwhile, put the egg yolks into a clean bowl and whisk in a stand mixer until they have doubled in volume. When the temperature of the sugar reaches 118°C, slowly pour the sugar into the eggs while whisking on a low speed, being careful to avoid the sides of the bowl and the whisk itself. Add the cherry reduction to the bowl while continuing to whisk until cool. Heat the remaining cream and mix in the bloomed gelatine. Fold this mixture through the eggs, then fold in the whipped cream. Decant the mixture into a piping bag and pipe into half-sphere silicone moulds. Arrange the toasted nibbed almonds on top to create what will be the base, and place in a blast chiller for 12 hours.

Almond Cream

1 litre whole milk
500g ground almonds
50ml Disaronno liqueur
1% Gellan F
Fine sea salt

Put the milk into a saucepan over a medium heat and bring to the boil. Add the ground almonds and a pinch of salt and allow to infuse for 30 minutes. When ready, pass the milk through a fine-meshed chinois and add the Disaronno. Weigh the liquid to calculate 1% of it, and add that amount of Gellan F. Transfer the mixture to a Thermomix and blend until the temperature reaches 90°C, then pour into a tray to set. When set, blend in the Thermomix a second time and pass through a fine-meshed drum sieve. Transfer to a squeezy bottle for service.

Chocolate Spray

To create an immaculate velvet finish on our parfaits and delices, we use a professional chocolate spray gun. In this case, 50% chocolate is mixed with 50% cocoa butter, then melted so that it is fluid enough to be sprayed onto the desserts. The delices must be sprayed as soon as they are taken out of the freezer so that the warm chocolate doesn't melt the mousse and ruin the perfect dome shape.

500g Valrhona Opalys white chocolate
500g cocoa butter, melted

Melt the chocolate and stir through the cocoa butter. Decant the mixture into a chocolate spray gun. Remove the parfaits from their moulds and spray chocolate all over, apart from the base. Return the parfaits to the freezer until service.

Cherry Gel

500g Boiron morello cherry purée
50ml Stock Syrup (see page 290)
15ml cherry vinegar
8g agar agar

Put the cherry purée, stock syrup and vinegar into a saucepan over a medium heat, whisk in the agar agar and bring to the boil for 2 minutes. Pour into a tray and place in the fridge to set. Once set, transfer the gel to a Vitamix and blend until smooth. Pass through a fine-meshed drum sieve, then pour into a squeezy bottle for service.

To Finish

Cherries, halved and stoned
Green almonds
Sweet cicely leaves
Oxalis leaves
Red-veined sorrel leaves
Sorrel flowers

Place a Cherry Parfait in the middle of each plate and arrange 5 cherry halves around three-quarters of the circumference, some standing up. Add various-sized dots of the Almond Cream and Cherry Gel. Garnish with 3 almonds and the herbs and flowers.

Dark Chocolate Delice, Raspberry, Biscuit Ice Cream

Like wine and coffee, chocolate can have a wide range of flavours and aromas, depending on the variety of cacao bean, where they are grown and how they are processed. In this delice, we use three different types of chocolate – mellow, malty Jivara (40% cacao), tart, fruity Manjari (64% cacao) and dark, bitter Guanaja (70%) – to create a complex and delicious dessert that is 100% indulgence.

Serves 8

Biscuit Ice Cream

65g digestive biscuits
500ml whole milk
165ml UHT cream
135g pasteurised egg yolks
80g caster sugar

Put the biscuits into a blender and blitz
to a fine crumb. Put the milk and cream
into a saucepan with the biscuit crumbs and
bring to the boil over a medium–high heat.
Meanwhile, whisk the egg yolks and caster
sugar together. Add a little of the hot milk
to the yolk mixture, then pour the mixture
into the saucepan. Reduce the heat and cook
until the temperature reaches 84°C, stirring
continuously. Chill over a bowl of iced water,
then pour into Pacojet beakers and freeze
before churning.

Raspberry Gel

500g Boiron raspberry purée
50ml Stock Syrup (see page 290)
10ml lemon juice
10g agar agar

Put the raspberry purée, stock syrup and
lemon juice into a saucepan over a medium–
high heat, whisk in the agar agar and bring
to the boil for 2 minutes. Pour into a tray and
place in the fridge to set. Transfer the gel
to a Vitamix and blend until smooth. Pass
through a fine-meshed drum sieve, then pour
into a squeezy bottle for service.

Crispy Chocolate Base

100g cocoa nibs
100g feuilletine
180g Valrhona Jivara chocolate, melted
30g cocoa butter, melted

Put the cocoa nibs and feuilletine into a
Thermomix and blitz to a fine powder. Add
the melted chocolate and cocoa butter and
blend together on the reverse setting until
combined. Pour the mixture onto a large sheet
of baking paper and cover with a second piece
of paper. Roll the mixture into a rectangular
shape 3mm thick, then place in the freezer.
Once frozen, cut into strips 12 × 3cm. Keep
frozen until needed.

Brownie Strips

75g soft unsalted butter
100g caster sugar
2 eggs
100g plain flour
1g bicarbonate of soda
1g baking powder
2g salt
10g cocoa powder
80g crème fraîche
10ml cabernet sauvignon vinegar
50g Valrhona Jivara chocolate, melted

Preheat the oven to 170°C fan. Put the sugar and butter into the bowl of a stand mixer and beat together until light and creamy. Continue to mix while adding 1 egg at a time, whisking until fully incorporated, then add the flour, bicarbonate of soda, baking powder, salt and cocoa powder. Once fully mixed, carefully fold in the crème fraîche, vinegar and melted chocolate. Pour into a high-sided, 30 × 20cm baking tray lined with baking paper. Place in the oven for 20 minutes. Allow to cool, then cut into strips 11.5 × 2.5cm.

Chocolate Mousse

10ml double cream
10g Marco Polo tea leaves (from Mariage Frères), finely blended
195g Valrhona Manjari dark chocolate
20g unsalted butter
2 egg yolks
4g cocoa powder
75ml grapeseed oil
115g pasteurised egg whites

Warm the cream over a low heat, then stir through the tea leaves. Put the chocolate, butter and flavoured cream into a bowl and place over a bain-marie to melt. Put the yolks, cocoa powder and 20ml water into a different bowl and mix together with a hand-held blender. Slowly add the oil while blending until emulsified. Put the egg whites into the bowl of a stand mixer and whisk to firm peaks. Fold the egg yolk mixture into the melted chocolate. Whisk in one-third of the egg whites by hand, then whisk in the rest. Transfer the mousse to a piping bag.

Chocolate Spray

250g Valrhona Guanaja chocolate
250g cocoa butter

Place the chocolate in a bowl over a bain-marie and allow to melt. Put the cocoa butter into a small saucepan and place over a low heat to melt. Once melted, stir the cocoa butter into the melted chocolate, then decant into a spray gun and keep warm.

Assembling the Delices

Pipe the Chocolate Mousse into rectangular delice moulds, then place a Brownie Strip on top, followed by a strip of the Crispy Chocolate Base. Place in the freezer for 12 hours. To finish, carefully pop the delices out of the moulds and cover with the Chocolate Spray while they are still frozen. Leave the delices to temper in the fridge for 4 hours.

Chocolate Decoration

Tempering is the process of heating and cooling chocolate to certain temperatures in order to stabilise the crystals in the cocoa butter. This ensures that the chocolate has a lovely shine and a satisfying snap when broken, while still being versatile enough to manipulate into decorations like this one.

250g Valrhona Manjari chocolate

Melt the chocolate in a bowl over a water bath heated to 55°C, stirring occasionally. Once it has melted and reached 55°C, place the bowl over an ice bath, stirring frequently and regularly checking the temperature. When the chocolate is between 28°C and 29°C, return the bowl to the warm water bath, stirring constantly until the temperature is between 31°C and 32°C. The chocolate is now tempered and can be poured onto an A4 acetate sheet. Spread with a large spatula until it is 2–3mm thick. Allow the chocolate to cool slightly, but before it sets hard, use a ruler and small knife to score strips 4mm wide across the sheet. Roll the sheet around a rolling pin at an angle so it is almost corner to corner, then fasten with sticky tape. Remove the rolling pin and place the chocolate cylinder in the fridge to set for 1 hour. Once the time has elapsed, remove the tape and allow the acetate sheet to unfurl. Remove the curved chocolate strips and store them on kitchen paper in an airtight container in the fridge until needed.

To Finish

Freeze-dried raspberry pieces
Gold leaf
Fresh raspberries, halved

Place a large dot of Raspberry Gel right of centre on a plate and cover with the freeze-dried raspberry pieces. Place a Dark Chocolate Delice and a Chocolate Decoration on the plate parallel with the raspberry pieces. Squeeze some dots of raspberry gel on top of the delice and put a small dot on top of the decoration. Stick a piece of gold leaf to that small dot, then place the raspberry halves up against the delice. Finally, place a rocher of Biscuit Ice Cream on the dried raspberry pieces.

Autumn

Despite autumn bringing a sense of the year winding down, it's impossible not to enjoy its golden sunshine and the spectacular array of colours on the trees. It feels like a last hurrah before winter hits us like a ton of bricks.

Inevitably, the range of produce available changes, with artichokes, courgettes and salad leaves giving way to heartier veg, such as carrots, Brussels sprouts, cabbage and pumpkin. Alongside them, lovely blackberries and apples continue to come in, then wild mushrooms begin to arrive. Among these are girolles, a highlight of the mushroom season, which we serve with spelt, black garlic and a smoked Cheddar velouté. We also take advantage of early chestnuts, which we smoke and use in our classic Mont Blanc with vanilla. Figs are another autumn gift, and it's a real pleasure to take delivery of wonderful black figs from Provence. These appear in our grilled lobster with verjus and coconut, a fantastic flavour combination.

Of course, the protein available during autumn changes too, and we start to get hold of some pretty special game, including grouse and deer. Pork too, although available all year round, really shines during autumn, and we often like to elevate everyday cuts into something spectacular. Côte de porc, or pork chop, for example, is delightful served with turnip purée, turnip ribbons, pickled walnut and Pommery mustard.

The ingredient shift we see in autumn is equally evident in terms of seafood and fish. Razor clams, native lobsters, cockles, spider crabs, turbot, cod, pollock and John Dory are all found in abundance. Among our favourite ways to serve John Dory is to gently fry it in beurre noisette until golden brown, then dust it with fennel powder and partner it with heirloom carrot purée, cockles and a vadouvan velouté.

There is much to celebrate during autumn, but weather and variations in growing conditions and the oceans inevitably affect what's available. This means we have to work with what the elements and environment allow, but always with a view to using the absolute best. It's a challenge for chefs when ingredient substitutions have to be made at short notice, but a source of stimulation too, as it requires the agility to make quick but well-informed decisions.

Inspirational ingredients

Figs
Wonderfully versatile, figs can be served raw, baked, candied, made into a confit in sugar syrup, preserved or turned into chutney. Fresh plump figs are both delicious to eat and visually alluring when sliced open. We sometimes offer them with baked cheese, or as a simple dessert drizzled with honey, but they also lend themselves to cakes, buns and pastries. Fig leaves too are extraordinary. They have a stunning depth of flavour and help to bring that quality to an array of dishes.

Among our favourite recipes that use both fruit and leaves is our autumn lobster dish, which is inspired by Thai green curry. We sit beautiful native lobster on top of a fig leaf, place it on the barbecue grill and allow it to gently warm through, absorbing the lovely fig leaf aroma, which is reminiscent of toasted coconut. To accompany this, we then take new-season figs, nigella and cumin and make something between a compote and a chutney. This plays on the sweetness of the fruit and is almost a riff on mango chutney. Alongside that is a lobster sauce, which starts with Thai aromatics – makrut lime leaves, lemongrass, ginger, garlic and shallots – and to these we add a touch of tomato purée and some dried chilli; in this case, dried chilli is preferred because it allows better flavour control than fresh chillies, which can be extremely variable. We then add a lobster reduction and coconut purée, and allow it to cook out until it resembles a Thai curry. Among the finishing touches are amaranth leaves, which add a sweet and nutty flavour, and fresh figs, which provide textural contrast. The Thai influence is evident, but the whole dish owes much more to the creativity of our chefs.

In addition, we sometimes dry fig leaves to make a powder for the flatbreads we serve with cheese, and we also add powdered fig leaves to the Parker House brioche and custard tarts we make, imbuing them with a subtle green colour, similar to matcha.

Game
Wild birds and animals, collectively known as game, are available on a strictly seasonal basis in the UK. The season opens in August, when grouse and snipe begin to appear, but the majority of game birds, including pheasant, duck, geese and partridge, become available

from September for roughly five months. The deer season lasts a similar amount of time, but the months vary according to the breed and sex of the deer. The restrictions on hunting ensure the longevity and sustainability of the species, and the limited period in which we can acquire game means that it always feels like a special treat.

Although we start serving grouse as soon as it becomes available – the Glorious Twelfth of August – we continue serving it throughout the autumn. The birds are shot and delivered to us complete with guts, but plucked to halfway down the shin, so they appear to be wearing little fluffy boots. Occasionally, we confit the thigh meat to add to a farce, but more often we use the legs, along with the wings, to make a sauce.

We prep the crown (ribcage with both breasts on) and poach it in seasoned chicken stock for 15 minutes. After that it is patted dry and fried in a mixture of hot oil, butter and thyme until the outside is nicely caramelised. As the skin can be a bit chewy, we always peel it off before serving, but it has helped to keep the breasts succulent. They are served with a grouse sauce containing blackberry liqueur and single malt whisky – just stunning!

Wild duck too is an amazing bird, full of flavour. We smoke ours and present it with a beautiful assortment of autumn produce, including beetroot, blackberries and hazelnuts. In fact, fruit works wonderfully with most types of game – apple with woodcock and quince with venison, for example – bringing balance and contrast to the often bold, rich flavours of the meat.

For many people, deer springs to mind whenever game is mentioned. There are several types of deer, and the venison that comes from them is a beautiful lean meat. We usually divide the saddle (long back joint) into its two loins and roast them, but sometimes we French-trim the eight-rib rack, and cook it like a rack of lamb, which we then serve as cutlets. The haunch, the muscular joint that comes from the top of the hind leg, is cut into steaks, which can be cooked medium rare and are beautifully tender.

Fallow deer leaps onto the menu in autumn and we serve the loin with slivers of new-season pumpkin, Brussels sprouts, and two sauces – pontack and grand veneur – which bring berry notes that provide a lovely contrast to the deeply flavoured meat. Sometimes we also cook Chinese water deer, an ornamental breed that lives by marshlands and has the best natural fat covering (almost a centimetre thick) of all the deer found in the UK. The saddle of this deer is small, about the size of a lamb saddle, and the first thing we do is to bone it.

We make a farce with the trimmings, some of the leg meat and a bit of pork fat, add shallots, thyme, cognac and white wine, and stuff the mixture inside the saddle. It's then rolled up and roasted over pine, which imparts a gentle woody flavour. We serve it carved into medallions, and the concentric circles of crisp fat, tender meat and herby stuffing look amazing in cross-section.

White truffles
At the beginning of autumn, we rely on Zac, our UK-based truffle man, to get us the best white truffles from his network of hunters and growers around the world. These days our supply comes from Istria in Croatia, and thanks to Zac we get fresh deliveries three times a week. This is really important, as the period between finding the truffle and serving it to the guest is as short as it possibly can be within a 48-hour window, which is essential to preserve its astounding quality and intoxicating aroma.

As white truffles are wild, rare and delicate, they must be handled and stored with great care. When a delivery arrives, we hand-select the truffles we want, always choosing the larger ones for shaving over finished dishes. Fundamentally, though, it's all about the nose. We smell each truffle one by one and select those that are the most aromatic. We are very pedantic about this.

The truffles are slightly dirty when they arrive, with sandy soil still clinging to them, but no cleaning happens at this point. We wrap our chosen truffles in kitchen paper and place them in a pine box, which allows them to breathe naturally; the last thing truffles want is a moist environment because that will cause them to sweat and deteriorate.

As and when we want a truffle, we select the right one for that service and ever so gently brush it with cool water, then use a metal spike to clean any remaining sand out of its tiny crevasses. After that it is gently dried.

White truffle enhances even the simplest of dishes. We like to shave it over freshly cooked pasta, spelt, scrambled egg or fried egg, where the warmth releases the truffle's fragrant notes and oils. Our lovely chestnut linguini certainly benefits from it. Chestnut flour is added to our basic linguini recipe, which is briefly cooked in boiling water, then tossed in a reduced chicken emulsion and served surrounded by a wonderful Parmesan and roasted garlic velouté. Fresh white truffle is shaved over it at the table – a simple but striking celebration of two fantastic autumn ingredients.

Truffle also makes a contribution to our take on a cheese fondue. We make a tarte fine in the shape of a ring and

dress it with caramelised onions, dill pickles and grilled onion petals. A fondue made with three different cheeses – Vacherin Mont d'Or, Cheddar and Gruyère – and yellow wine from the Jura region is poured into the middle of the tarte by the waiters at the table, then white truffle is shaved over the top. It's amazing theatre for the guest, and the aromas and flavours are out of this world.

Quince

This is a fruit loved by our chefs for its vibrant colour and incredible flavour. They hover around the delivery, trying to grab one of the ripe fruits so they can inhale its sweet, intoxicating perfume. The aromatics in the skin are extraordinary, so whether we are poaching the fruit or making a purée or sorbet, we always start by making a syrup in which the peel infuses for about 20 minutes. After that, the quince flesh is vacuum-packed in the syrup and cooked in a water bath for 12 hours, during which time it turns a deep burgundy colour, like that of quince paste.

If necessary, quince can be cooked in about 20 minutes, but the flesh will remain slightly golden rather than glowing red, and be a little al dente. We prefer a longer cooking time to get the deep colour and bring out all the natural sugars too. We use the cooked fruit in segments, or blend it with the syrup to make a beautiful purée or sorbet. The latter is served with a heather honey mousse and a spiced tuille 'lid', which the guest has to break through to get to the cream and sorbet. It's as lovely to look at as it is to eat.

Quinces are under-used in the UK, perhaps because they are still somewhat unusual and many people are not sure what to do with them. This is a pity because the cooked fruit has a wonderful texture and is able to carry other flavours, such as vanilla, herbs and spices. It makes a delicious contribution to autumn, which truly can be a thrilling gastronomic season.

Grilled Lobster, Black Fig, Verjus, Coconut

Although lobster is traditionally paired with sharp citrus, often lemon or lime, sweeter fruits, such as cherries, mango and figs, also work beautifully with the sweet shellfish. The observation that fig leaves taste mildly of coconut led to this unexpected combination of lobster, figs and a mildly spiced coconut sauce. Verjus gel and dashi vinegar contrast with the sweetness so that the finished dish is well balanced and completely delicious.

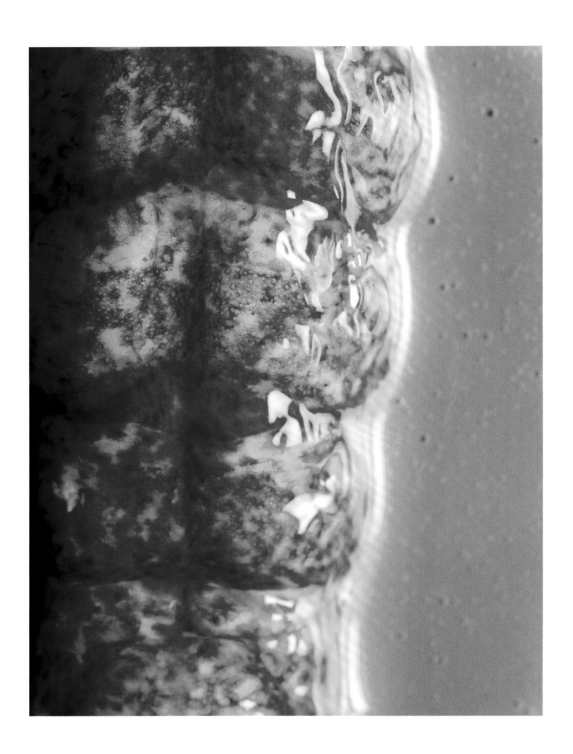

Serves 8

Lobster Coconut Sauce

Vegetable oil
2 shallots, peeled and finely sliced
40g ginger, peeled and grated
2 garlic cloves, peeled and roughly chopped
2 makrut lime leaves
3 fig leaves, roughly chopped
1g piment d'Espelette chilli powder
1 lemongrass stick, bashed and chopped
25g tomato purée
125g coconut purée
125ml Lobster Reduction (see page 230)
100ml Chicken Stock (see page 289)
200ml whole milk
100ml double cream
50g crème fraîche
Fine sea salt

Place a large saucepan over a medium heat and add a drizzle of oil. When hot, add the shallots, ginger, garlic, makrut lime leaves and fig leaves, piment d'Espelette and lemongrass, season with salt and sweat until aromatic. Add the tomato purée and cook for 30 seconds, then add the coconut purée, lobster reduction, chicken stock, milk and cream. Bring to the boil and allow to simmer for 30 minutes. Pass through a fine-meshed chinois. Add the crème fraîche and incorporate using a hand-held blender. Adjust the seasoning, if necessary. Cool and store in the fridge until needed.

Fig Chutney

500g black figs, finely diced
100g muscovado sugar
150g beetroot, peeled and coarsely grated
150g shallots, peeled and finely diced
15g ginger, peeled and finely sliced
200ml chardonnay vinegar
10g toasted nigella seeds
10g toasted cumin seeds
20ml cranberry vinegar

Put all the ingredients, except the cranberry vinegar, into a saucepan and season with salt. Place over a medium heat and bring to the boil, then allow to simmer for about 1 hour, until thickened. Adjust the seasoning, if necessary, and add the cranberry vinegar. Allow to cool, then store in the fridge.

Verjus Gel

300g verjus
100g Stock Syrup (see page 290)
12g agar agar

Place the verjus, stock syrup and 200ml water in a small saucepan over a medium heat, whisk in the agar agar and bring to the boil for 2 minutes. Pour into a tray and place in the fridge to set. Once set, transfer the gel to a Vitamix and blend until smooth. Pass through a fine-meshed drum sieve, then pour into a squeezy bottle for service.

Lobster

8 × 500g native lobsters
100ml white wine vinegar

Put the lobsters into the freezer for 30 minutes prior to preparing. Add the vinegar to a large saucepan of water and bring to the boil. Wearing kitchen gloves, separate the lobster tail from the body, then remove the claws, reserving them to make lobster oil (see page 119). Now pinch the middle fin of the tail and twist carefully, pulling out the entrails; if unsuccessful, use kitchen pliers to remove them. Insert 2 long wooden skewers down the back of the tails so they are straight. Blanch the tails in the boiling water for 2½ minutes. Remove from the pan and allow to cool at room temperature for 2 minutes before removing the skewers. Using scissors or the back of a heavy knife, carefully crack the shell to remove it from the tail, reserving the shells for the oil. Trim a little off the body end of the tail to neaten. Place the tails on a tray lined with kitchen paper and store in the fridge until required.

To Finish

Dashi Vinegar Glaze (see page 119)
Lobster Oil (see page 119)
Amaranth leaves
Oxalis leaves
Sorrel flowers
Black fig wedges

Prepare and light a Japanese konro grill. Insert 2 yakitori skewers through each Lobster from tail to head. Brush each tail with the dashi vinegar glaze and drizzle with lobster oil. Place on the grill and cook for 6 minutes, turning frequently until the tails have warmed through, then remove the skewers. Gently warm the Fig Chutney and place a large quenelle left of centre on each plate. Place 3 fig wedges on the chutney and dot with the Verjus Gel. Garnish with the leaves and flowers. Place the lobster on the plate. Warm the Lobster Coconut Sauce and serve at the table.

Autumnal Salad, Smoked Duck, Beetroot, Blackberries, Hazelnut

This salad changes throughout autumn, depending on what vegetables, leaves and fruits come in from our suppliers, but it always includes smoked duck breast, duck hearts, baby beetroot and toasted hazelnuts. Here we have added pickled blackberries, shimeji mushrooms, shallot rings, purple oxalis and red amaranth leaves for a stunning combination of colours, tastes and textures, and a dish that echoes the changing leaves of the season.

Serves 8

Elderflower Vinegar

To extend the season of elderflowers, we make this vinegar, and the Elderflower Honey on page 152, when the blooms are at their freshest in spring, preserving their wonderful flavour for the rest of the year.

> 100g fresh elderflower heads
> 500ml chardonnay vinegar

Put the elderflower heads into a Kilner jar and cover with the vinegar. Place the jar in the fridge and allow to infuse for a minimum of 1 week before using.

Grilled Duck Hearts

> 300g duck hearts
> 30g fine sea salt
> 2 tbsp duck fat

Clean and trim the duck hearts, then mix them with the salt and leave for 2 hours. Rinse under running cold water for a good 20 minutes, then pat them dry on kitchen paper. Place in a sous-vide bag with the duck fat and seal under vacuum. Heat a water bath to 60°C and place the bag in it for 3 hours. Chill in an ice bath and set aside until needed.

Pickled Wild Blackberries

> 100g wild blackberries
> 25ml cranberry vinegar
> 25ml Stock Syrup (see page 290)

Combine all the ingredients in a sous-vide bag and seal under vacuum. Heat a water bath to 50°C and place the bag in it for 2 hours. Chill in an ice bath and set aside until needed.

Baby Beetroot

> 500g baby red beetroots, washed
> 500g baby golden beetroots, washed
> Olive oil
> 2 thyme sprigs
> 2 garlic cloves, cracked with the blade
>   of a chef's knife
> 75ml white balsamic vinegar
> 200ml beetroot juice
> Fine sea salt

Preheat the oven to 180°C no fan. Place 2 large rectangular sheets of foil on a baking tray and a smaller square sheet of baking paper on top. Season the beetroots with olive oil and salt, then place them on the paper with the thyme and garlic. Wrap them tightly in the foil to create a sealed parcel. Bake in the oven for 45 minutes, or until tender. While still warm, carefully peel off the skin and trim the bottoms neatly, leaving the roots on if possible. Cut any larger beets in half. Mix the white balsamic vinegar and beetroot juice together in a bowl, add the beetroots and allow to marinate for a minimum of 30 minutes. Store in the fridge until needed.

Herb Cream

> 200g crème fraîche
> 50ml UHT cream
> 4g fine sea salt
> 20g Herb Purée (see page 84)
> 5g Ultratex

Mix all the ingredients together and allow to infuse in the fridge for 30 minutes. Pass through a fine-meshed drum sieve, then transfer to a squeezy bottle and keep cold until needed.

Blackberry Gel

> 500g Boiron blackberry purée
> 50ml Stock Syrup (see page 290)
> 10ml blackberry vinegar
> 20ml crème de mûre
> 7g agar agar

Put the blackberry purée, stock syrup, vinegar and crème de mûre into a saucepan over a medium–high heat, whisk in the agar agar and bring to the boil for 2 minutes. Pour into a tray and place in the fridge to set. Once set, transfer the gel to a Vitamix and blend until smooth. Pass through a fine-meshed drum sieve, then pour into a squeezy bottle and set aside until needed.

Pickled Shimeji Mushrooms

> 150g shimeji mushrooms
> 50ml hazelnut oil
> 15ml Pedro Ximénez sherry vinegar

Using kitchen scissors, trim the mushrooms so all the stems are 1cm long. Put them into a small saucepan with the hazelnut oil and season with salt. Place over a medium–high heat and bring to the boil. Remove from the heat, add the PX vinegar and allow to cool. Once cooled, store in the fridge until needed.

Hazelnut and Elderflower Dressing

> 80ml Elderflower Vinegar (see top left)
> 20g Elderflower Honey (see page 152)
> 15g Dijon mustard
> 150ml hazelnut oil
> Freshly ground black pepper

Put all the ingredients into a bowl, add some salt and blitz together with a hand-held blender. Decant into a squeezy bottle and set aside until needed.

To Finish

> Sliced smoked duck
> Pickled Shallot Rings (see page 149)
> Roasted hazelnuts
> Sobacha
> Red amaranth leaves
> Small nasturtium leaves
> Purple oxalis leaves
> Red-veined sorrel leaves
> Sorrel flowers
> Chive tips

Place a frying pan over a high heat. Once hot, dry-fry the Grilled Duck Hearts until caramelised and warmed through, then slice them in half lengthways. Dress the Baby Beetroot with the Hazelnut and Elderflower Dressing. Build the salads in 10cm rings in the middle of your bowls. Start with various-sized dots of the Herb Cream and Blackberry Gel. Add the beetroots, 5 slices of smoked duck and 3 pieces of heart, then garnish the salad with the pickled shallot rings, Pickled Shimeji Mushrooms, hazelnuts, sobacha, the various leaves, flowers and chive tips.

Chestnut Linguine, Aged Parmesan, White Truffle

A twist of fresh chestnut-flavoured linguine is hidden in a mist of Parmesan velouté that has been aerated to create a light but intense foam. Chestnut flour in the dough changes the colour of the finished pasta from yellow to a pale beige. It also adds a sweet nuttiness that works really well with the white truffle that is shaved over the top at the table, perhaps because chestnuts and white truffles are in season at exactly the same time.

Serves 8

Chestnut Linguine

The amount of egg needed to bring the dough together changes each time we make this pasta, so it's important not to add it all at once. Instead, we pour it in a steady stream and test regularly by taking a pinch of the mixture between two fingers and rubbing them together; if it isn't dry and powdery and sticks together to form a soft dough, it's ready.

> 4 large eggs, plus 6 large egg yolks
> 450g '00' flour, plus extra for dusting
> 100g chestnut flour
> 2g fine sea salt

Crack the whole eggs into a bowl, add the yolks and whisk until combined. Put the '00' flour, chestnut flour and salt into a Robot Coupe and, with the machine running, slowly add the eggs until the dough resembles breadcrumbs. When the consistency is correct, bring the dough together by hand and transfer it to a floured surface. Knead for 1–2 minutes, until it begins to show some elasticity, then wrap it tightly in cling film. Put the dough into the fridge to rest for at least 1 hour. After that, allow it to sit at room temperature for 20–30 minutes before rolling out. Using a rolling pin, roll the dough into a thin sheet, then pass it through the pasta machine on the widest setting. Pass it through the machine a few more times, increasing the setting by two each time, until it is halfway down the settings. Fold the ends into the middle and pass the dough through the machine again from the widest setting to the middle setting. Repeat this step 3 more times to work the gluten, then increase the setting and pass the dough through the machine until it is approximately 3mm thick. Use the linguine attachment to cut the pasta into thin strips, then store them in the fridge until needed.

Parmesan Velouté

> ½ garlic bulb
> 2 banana shallots, sliced
> 1 thyme sprig
> 5 white peppercorns
> 500ml Chicken Stock (see page 289)
> 500ml whole milk
> 500ml double cream
> 250g aged Parmesan, grated
> 25g soya lecithin
> Fine sea salt

Preheat the oven to 180°C fan. Wrap the garlic in foil and place in the oven for 30–45 minutes, until soft. Put the shallots, thyme and peppercorns into a saucepan and cover with the chicken stock. Place the pan over a medium–high heat, bring to the boil and reduce the liquid by half. Add the milk and cream and return to the boil. Remove the garlic from the foil and squeeze the flesh out of the skin before adding it to the saucepan with the grated cheese. Remove from the heat and allow to infuse for 30 minutes. Pass through a fine-meshed chinois into a clean pan and season with salt. Stir through the soya lecithin and set aside until needed.

To Finish

> 75ml Chicken Stock (see page 289)
> 25g unsalted butter
> Aged Parmesan, grated
> Barolo vinegar
> White truffle

Heat the chicken stock in a saucepan over a medium heat, then add the butter. When melted, use a hand-held blender to emulsify. Divide the Chestnut Linguine into 4 and cook each portion in boiling salted water for 1 minute. For each of the 4 portions, bring 25ml of the chicken stock emulsion to the boil in a saucepan and allow to reduce slightly. Add the pasta with a handful of grated aged Parmesan and a splash of Barolo vinegar and toss to coat. Using a pair of tongs, twist half of each portion into a neat beehive and place in the middle of a warm plate. Aerate the Parmesan Velouté until foaming, then spoon over the pasta. Finish by shaving fresh white truffle over the top.

Spelt, Girolles, Smoked Montgomery Cheddar, Black Garlic

Wild and cultivated mushrooms are key ingredients in autumn, and we use a combination to give depth to this spelt dish. A stock made with field mushrooms and ceps, and flavoured with garlic, thyme and Madeira, is the base of the 'risotto', which is served with sautéd girolles and cep-flavoured puffed spelt. Dots of black garlic and green herb purées add textural and visual contrast, and a smoked Cheddar velouté finishes the dish in the form of a delicate foam.

Serves 8

Mushroom Stock

1kg flat mushrooms, roughly chopped
5 shallots, peeled and sliced
3 garlic cloves, cracked with the blade
   of a chef's knife
100g dried ceps
10 thyme sprigs
350ml dry Madeira

Put all the ingredients into a large saucepan and cover with cold water. Place over a high heat and bring to the boil. Reduce the heat and simmer for 2 hours. Pass through a fine-meshed chinois, being sure to squeeze out all the liquid. Allow to cool, then store in the fridge until required.

Smoked Montgomery Cheddar Velouté

Just before serving, we aerate the velouté to create a light foam. To help stabilise this foam so that it reaches the table without collapsing, we add soya lecithin, an emulsifier that gives the sauce structure and helps the bubbles to last longer.

500ml Chicken Stock (see page 289)
2 shallots, peeled and finely sliced
½ bay leaf
6 white peppercorns
1 garlic clove, cracked with the blade
   of a chef's knife
1 thyme sprig
250ml double cream
250ml whole milk
250g smoked Montgomery Cheddar,
   grated
15g soya lecithin
Fine sea salt

Put the chicken stock into a saucepan and add the shallots, bay leaf, white peppercorns, garlic and thyme. Season with salt, bring to the boil and allow to reduce by half. Once reduced, add the cream and milk and return to the boil. Take the pan off the heat, add the Cheddar and stir to melt. Cover the pan with cling film and allow to infuse; do not return to the heat or it will become grainy. After 20 minutes, pass the sauce through a fine-meshed chinois and add the soya lecithin. Mix together with a hand-held blender, then adjust the seasoning, if necessary. Allow to cool before storing in the fridge.

Shallot Confit

Olive oil
4 banana shallots, peeled and finely diced
1 thyme sprig

Place a small saucepan over a medium heat. Once warm, add a little oil, then add the shallots and season with salt. Sweat without colouring for 5 minutes, until the shallots are translucent. Add the thyme and enough olive oil to just cover the shallots. Cover with a cartouche and cook on the lowest possible heat for 30 minutes, until the shallots are sweet and very soft. Allow to cool, then store in the fridge until needed.

Sautéd Girolles

200g baby girolles
Olive oil
50g Garlic and Parsley Butter (see page 59)

Using a turning knife, gently scrape the mushroom stalks, discarding the peelings, then trim the bases, leaving a 1cm stalk. Thoroughly wash the mushrooms in cold water to remove any dirt and woodland grit, then allow to dry on kitchen paper for 30 minutes. Next, place a medium-sized sauté pan over a medium heat. Once warm, add a little olive oil and gently sauté the girolles. Lightly season with salt, then add the garlic and parsley butter. Turn the heat up and continue to cook until the butter is foaming. Adjust the seasoning, if necessary, then set aside for service.

Puffed Spelt

100g spelt
10g dried cep powder

Heat a deep-fat fryer to 180°C. When hot, add the spelt grains and cook until they stop bubbling. Transfer to a bowl, add the cep powder and season with salt. Spread the grains out on a tray lined with kitchen paper and keep warm.

Toasted Spelt

30ml olive oil
500g spelt
40g Shallot Confit (see near left)
200ml white wine
1.5 litres Mushroom Stock (see far left)

Place a saucepan over a medium–high heat, then add the olive oil and spelt and toast for 2 minutes. Add the shallot confit and wine and stir continuously until the wine has reduced. Once reduced, add the mushroom stock and bring to the boil. Reduce the heat to a gentle simmer and cook for about 10 minutes, until the spelt is tender. The stock should all be absorbed by this point. Season with salt, then transfer to a shallow container and cool in a blast chiller for 10 minutes. Place in the fridge until required.

To Finish

Cold unsalted butter cubes
Crème fraîche
Aged Parmesan, finely grated
Aged malt vinegar
Black Garlic Purée (see page 148)
Herb Purée (see page 84)
Baby rocket leaves
Mustard leaves
Allium buds

Put the Toasted Spelt mixture into a medium-sized saucepan, add 6 cubes of butter and just enough Mushroom Stock to cover. Place over a medium–high heat and bring to the boil. Keep boiling until the stock has evaporated and the spelt is hot. Remove from the heat and add another 4 cubes of butter, a tablespoon of crème fraîche, some grated Parmesan and a little splash of vinegar. Beat well and adjust the seasoning, if necessary. Place the spelt mixture in the middle of a bowl and flatten. Spoon over the Sautéd Girolles, add dots of the black garlic and herb purées, then scatter over some Puffed Spelt and garnish with the leaves and flowers. Warm the Smoked Montgomery Cheddar Velouté, then use a hand-held blender to make it fluffy. Spoon the velouté around the spelt.

HARD GRAFT AND GLAMOUR

Many people think success is all glory and glamour. Let me tell you, there's a big downside as well. You only have to pick up a newspaper or go online to find some sort of mud-flinging, and I've been part of it – from very public personal spats and arguments about kitchen culture to vegan protests in the restaurant. The world moves at a really fast pace, and when you reach a certain level of notoriety, any misstep or wrong word can make you an easy target. My view is that it's all character-building.

Professional kitchens never have been, and never will be, for lightweights. They are tough places where you must work damned hard to make it. Nevertheless, the culture has changed, becoming less aggressive, more collaborative, and rightly so. Rather like sporting teams, restaurant kitchens require everyone to be on the same page and, importantly, to have each other's back. The level of commitment within a team is extraordinary. It means long days, an overload of adrenalin and ultimately a crash, but those who stick with it find an environment in which they learn and thrive.

I remember Marco Pierre White's theory that all good food comes out of small kitchens, but maybe that sprang from the fact that the one at Harvey's was hardly big enough to swing a ladle. It had a table in it that served as the kitchen hotplate, but after service Steve Terry and I had to take it outside so we had more space to work. Of course, it makes sense to get the most out of the space you have. Rather like the perfect plate of food, nothing is wasted and every element is maximised.

The kitchen at Royal Hospital Road isn't very big either, but it does work efficiently, if somewhat frenziedly. The calmness in the dining room belies the tension behind the scenes, where staff have gone to amazing lengths over the years to ensure every one of our guests has the night of their life. The kitchen is a hothouse in every sense of the word, so things do sometimes go wrong and have to be coped with. Perhaps a tray of sea bass is dropped on the floor and ruined for service, or a giant pot of hot stock gets spilled and scalds a chef's ankles. Kitchen equipment too can go down at any time. It feels almost weekly that we have a repair person in to get a fridge or stove back into action, forcing the brigade to manoeuvre around them as they try to go about their own work.

Back in the early days of Restaurant Gordon Ramsay, I'd go into the restaurant on a Sunday to check if the fridges were working and to make sure we were ready for the week ahead. Being closed at weekends meant that Mondays were always extremely busy for everyone, with deliveries streaming through the back door, prep happening frantically at every work station, and people multi-tasking like crazy.

Beneath the restaurant is a rabbit warren of cool-rooms, dry-stores, offices and cellars. It's like the secret dens of MI5 down there, and the ceilings are so low that anyone over 6ft tall can't stand up straight. One night, while taking stock and having a glass of wine, I was overcome by tiredness, because we'd lost some staff and were down to eight in the kitchen (a third of what was required on a normal service). I simply fell asleep in the wine cellar. It was darker than usual as some of the lights weren't working, and the next thing I knew was waking up at 5.30am with half a glass of red wine still in my hand. That's the problem when you're a chef. The job takes such a toll that the moment you stop, bang, you're out cold.

Down beneath the restaurant on a Sunday was my favourite place to plan how I would motivate the team to get through to Wednesday night, by which point we'd have broken the back of the week. We'd have worked 18-hour days to get there, but Thursday and Friday would feel like a doddle in comparison – we were on the home straight.

I'd rise very early on Monday and always be first in the kitchen. I knew the value of setting a good example, especially if I expected the team to believe in my vision. Mark Askew, my head chef, was second to come in, and on this particular day I noticed he was limping. I said nothing at the time, but a bit later he caught me looking at him, so suddenly stopped limping and straightened up.

'Mark, why are you limping?' I asked.

'No, I'm good. I'm not limping,' he replied.

'You are limping massively,' I pointed out.

'No, I'm fine, Chef,' he said.

'Mark, tell me, what the hell is going on?'

'Well, I had a motorbike accident on Friday night,' he said, lowering his chef pants so I could see he was black and blue from the top of his thigh right down to his ankle. The reason soon became clear ...

Friday night used to be the big clean-down in the kitchen because we would be closed on Saturday and Sunday. Apparently, Mark had been cleaning until 2.30am, and then, because it was the last night of the month, he started stock-taking to work out our requirements when all the fresh produce began arriving on Monday. He ended up leaving the restaurant, dog-tired, about 3.30am. He jumped on his motorbike and started to head home, but fell asleep and rode into a side railing. A lesser mortal would have called for help, but he simply got up, walked home and came into work on Monday without mentioning it. He didn't want to let the team down by taking time off. That selflessness was ingrained in our culture.

These days, after a nasty accident like Mark's, I reckon chefs would take at least two weeks off to get fixed, and rightly so. You can show commitment without doing yourself permanent damage. But back then, that kind of attitude, strength and determination were admired, perhaps expected. Restaurant life was tough across the board and you had to commit all or nothing. Sometimes, though, the body blacks out, and that's exactly what happened to Mark.

It's hard to describe the commitment you feel to each other in the team, but for any aspiring chef, finding the right team is a must. The other essential is finding the right kitchen in which to learn, progress and master your craft. Not for nothing is the kitchen team referred to as a brigade. The comradeship and sense of unity in reaching for a desired goal are more generally found in a military context.

I thought I knew everything about cooking when I walked into Marco Pierre White's kitchen at Harvey's, but it was entirely different from what I'd experienced before. I had been a hotel chef, where I'd wasted my time entering what are scathingly called the Jelly Olympics – competitions to win some minor award. To get on as I wanted, I should have been finding a mentor to push me to unheard of levels, but I became distracted by easy wins.

On one occasion, I competed at Hotel Olympia in Kensington, where I did a canapé of salmon topped with pieces of lobster set in aspic. Aspic was the go-to savoury meat gelatine made from consommé, which at that time I thought was the peak of gastronomy. I basically cut a slice of bread into rounds, spread them with a salmon mousse, then placed a piece of wobbly aspic jelly lobster on top. My effort, the sort of canapé you'd only see somewhere like Buckingham Palace today, won me a gold certificate. This is cheffing, I thought, ignoring the fact that it looked good but tasted dreadful.

I was brought down with a thump when I later walked into the kitchen at Harvey's. Carrying my rolled-up knives and one of my awards, I was keen as mustard to impress. Marco looked at me and asked. 'What have you got there?'

'I have a gold certificate,' I replied.

He looked at it and laughed. We still laugh about it now. How embarrassing, a gold bloody certificate for a meat glue aspic lobster!

These days Marco and I talk more than ever before. I guess we've both grown up, and we look back and laugh at so many moments. He also ribs me about some of my ventures. After going into one of my Street Burger venues, he sent me a message saying, 'I should be delivering these for you, boy.' I don't mind a bit that he still calls me 'boy' because it's said tongue in cheek, reminding me that he was once my mentor.

I remember having my own laugh on a young American chef who'd come to work at Aubergine. When I asked what he thought about the restaurant scene in London, he went on at some length about how dated British food was and what a terrible reputation it had. His words struck me as arrogant and condescending, not a good start on his very first day. 'Does he want a job here?' I wondered. 'Why has he chosen London to learn his craft?'

I decided to play a joke on him, so I grabbed the expensive Gucci loafers he'd left downstairs and set them in a plant pot with the strongest aspic I could make –about 150 leaves of gelatin and 2 litres of chicken stock. Once set, I smashed the pot and gave him his moulded loafers back. Everyone had a good laugh, and even he found it funny. I should add that using aspic like this is all it's good for. You might as well be eating a loafer.

Mentoring is a part of my job that I've always enjoyed, an opportunity to guide and influence others who find food as inspiring as I do. I have time to do even more of it now, and it's not just with my staff. Hollywood came calling when they wanted a three-star chef to help them deliver a realistic representation of a top restaurant in the film *Burnt*. And when Bradley Cooper was researching his role in that movie, he spent some time at Restaurant Gordon Ramsay to understand what it's like to work in such a place. Among the things I taught him were how to dress a plate in 90 seconds.

'Use the plate like a clock face,' I told him, 'and don't let artistic expression override common sense. You must remember people are eating this and it's really annoying if ingredients are too close to the edge and fall off the plate. You also need to work quickly because the temperature of the protein ingredient is dropping every ten seconds.'

Bradley was a great student. He took on board everything he'd learned in the kitchen and really captured the essence of what it takes to be a professional chef. The result on film was amazingly realistic.

Part of Bradley's 'training' involved dining with me at Restaurant Gordon Ramsay so he could understand how the chefs' attention to detail manifests in an elegant dining experience. We had a wonderful dinner, but I'm a chef at heart and belong in the kitchen, not the dining room. I love the fact that I have created an exquisite and elegant dining experience, but the joy for me lies in providing that magic, not in eating it.

I have a similar feeling when I treat myself to a bottle selected from the restaurant's stunning wine list, which we've put together over the last 20 years at substantial expense. I prefer to enjoy it behind closed doors rather than in the restaurant.

I've asked myself why I feel like this, and think there are two main reasons. One is that I still have the mentality of an employee. Restaurant Gordon Ramsay wasn't created for me to indulge myself with lavish dining experiences; it was built to deliver an evening that guests will never forget. The other reason is that I am still a boy from a council estate, where food was sustenance rather than elegance, so I'm not really at ease in glamorous surroundings.

It's odd, I know, but such is the life of a chef.

John Dory, Heirloom Carrots, Fennel, Cockles, Vadouvan

Vadouvan is a French colonial spice mix that includes dehydrated onions, shallots and garlic, as well as dried spices. These give it a sweetness and pungency that brings a beautiful fragrance and gentle warmth to the creamy carrot velouté that is poured over the pollen-dusted John Dory fillet before serving. Like garam masala, vadouvan recipes vary greatly, but they always include cumin, mustard and fenugreek seeds for a distinctive aromatic sweetness and mild warmth.

Serves 8

Vadouvan Spice Mix

Vegetable oil
450g onions, peeled and finely sliced
250g shallots, peeled and finely sliced
6 garlic cloves, peeled and chopped
5g fenugreek seeds
15g cumin seeds
5g cardamom pods
5g yellow mustard seeds
5g turmeric powder
5g nutmeg, freshly grated
2g chilli flakes
2g whole cloves
12 fresh curry leaves
Fine sea salt

Place a large, heavy-based saucepan over a medium–high heat and pour in a little oil. When hot, add the onions, shallots and garlic, then season with salt. Sweat, stirring regularly, for 20 minutes, until caramelised. Add the spices to the caramelised onions and stir to combine. Continue to sweat for 30 minutes, until aromatic. Spread the spiced onions over a tray lined with baking paper, then place in a dehydrator heated to 75°C and leave for 12 hours. After the time has elapsed, store in an airtight container.

Fennel Powder

200g fennel fronds
20g fennel pollen

Carefully lay the fennel tops on trays lined with baking paper, then place in a dehydrator heated to 70°C and leave overnight. When dried, transfer to a Vitamix, add the fennel pollen and blend to a powder. Transfer to an icing duster for service.

Vadouvan Velouté

250g unsalted butter
2 large carrots, peeled and grated
20g Vadouvan Spice Mix (see left)
500ml Chicken Stock (see page 289)
250ml double cream
125ml whole milk
50g Carrot Purée (see page 70)
100g crème fraîche

Put the butter into a large, heavy-based saucepan over a medium heat. When the butter has melted, add the grated carrots and vadouvan, season with salt, then sweat for 20 minutes, until the carrots look pale and the butter is a rich orange-yellow colour. Add the chicken stock, bring to the boil and allow to reduce by half. Add the cream and milk and return to the boil. Once boiling, set aside to infuse for 20 minutes. Pass through a fine-meshed chinois, discarding the carrots. Add the carrot purée and crème fraîche and blitz together using a hand-held blender. Adjust the seasoning, if necessary, then chill until needed.

Cockles

300g cockles, purged

Bring a medium-sized saucepan of salted water to the boil. Blanch the cockles in it for 30 seconds, until they are open, then plunge into iced water to cool for 2 minutes. Remove the cockles from their shells and use kitchen scissors to cut off the entrails. Wash under cold running water, pat dry with kitchen paper and store in the fridge until needed.

Heirloom Carrots

Olive oil
8 purple Chantenay carrots, peeled and trimmed
8 yellow Chantenay carrots, peeled and trimmed
8 orange Chantenay carrots, peeled and trimmed
225ml Chicken Stock (see page 289)
15g unsalted butter

Place three small sauté pans with lids over a medium heat. Once warm, add a little oil and place a different colour of carrots in each one. Season with salt and gently sauté for 30 seconds, then add 75ml of the chicken stock to each pan. Place the lids on the pans and cook for 3 minutes, until the carrots are tender. Remove the lids and add 5g of the butter to each pan, stirring to create an emulsion with the cooking juices. Adjust the seasoning, if necessary, and transfer to trays to cool. Set aside until required.

John Dory

4 John Dory fillets, skinned
Beurre Noisette (see page 289)

Using a sharp knife, separate the fillets into the three muscles, trimming off any sinews. When ready to cook, place a large non-stick frying pan over a medium–high heat. Add a little beurre noisette, gently season the fish portions with salt, and place, skin-side down, in the pan. Place a cook's weight on top and fry until the edges turn golden brown. Once evenly caramelised, turn the portions over and cook for a further 30 seconds. Remove from the pan and trim the points of the fillets at an angle. Keep warm for service.

To Finish

Lime zest
Pickled Carrot Ribbons (see page 70)
Baby Fennel (see page 70)
Carrot Purée (see page 70)
Carrot tops
Fennel tops
Bronze fennel
Fennel flowers
Coriander flowers
Flaky sea salt

Dust the John Dory fillets with the Fennel Powder, season with some flaky sea salt and add a little lime zest. Arrange the different coloured Heirloom Carrots on a plate; between these add the pickled carrot ribbons, baby fennel and dots of warmed carrot purée. Next, add the warmed Cockles and garnish with the leaves and flowers. Place the fish next to the garnish and serve with the warmed Vadouvan Velouté on the side.

Aynhoe Park Fallow Deer, Pumpkin, Sprouts, Pontack, Grand Veneur Sauce

Beautifully pink fillets of fallow deer from Aynhoe Park in Northamptonshire are accompanied by golden discs of violina pumpkin, blanched and crispy sprout leaves and pontack sauce, which is made from ripe elderberries spiced with cloves and allspice. An indulgent grand veneur or 'huntsman' sauce flavoured with redcurrant jelly and dark chocolate is poured over the dish at the table.

Serves 8

Pontack

500g ripe elderberries, stems removed
500ml apple cider vinegar
200g shallots, peeled and finely sliced
5 cloves
5 allspice berries
1 tsp freshly grated nutmeg
1 tsp freshly ground black pepper
75g caster sugar
½ tsp fine sea salt
40g Ultratex

Preheat the oven to 120°C fan. Put the elderberries and vinegar into an ovenproof saucepan, cover tightly with foil and place in the oven for 8 hours. After the time has elapsed, remove from the oven and discard the foil. Add all the remaining ingredients, apart from the Ultratex, then place the saucepan over a medium heat and bring to the boil. Reduce the heat and allow to simmer for 30 minutes. Set aside to cool slightly before transferring to a Vitamix. Add the Ultratex and blend until smooth. Pass through a fine-meshed drum sieve and allow to cool. Once cool, pour into sterilised jars and leave for 2 days. When needed, transfer to a squeezy bottle for service.

Deer Loins

1 fallow deer saddle
Vegetable oil
Unsalted butter
Fine sea salt

Remove the inner fillets from the saddle and set aside for the sauce. Remove the 2 large loins, trimming off any sinew, then cut each loin into 4 equal portions. Reserve all the trimmings and bones for the sauce. For service, preheat the oven to 200°C fan. Place a cast-iron pan over a high heat, add a little oil and season the deer loins with salt. When the pan is smoking hot, sear the loins for 1 minute on each side, treating each loin as a cuboid with 4 sides. Add a knob of butter to the pan and, when it foams, baste the deer with it while turning the meat continuously for 1 minute. Transfer to a wire rack over a roasting tray and place in the oven for 3 minutes. Turn the loins over and cook for a further 3 minutes. Remove from the oven and allow to rest for 10 minutes.

Grand Veneur Sauce

1kg deer bones, chopped
Vegetable oil
1kg deer trimmings, roughly chopped
1 large onion, peeled and diced
1 large carrot, peeled and diced
2 celery sticks, diced
3 garlic cloves, cracked with the blade of a chef's knife
10 black peppercorns, crushed
10 juniper berries, crushed
½ bay leaf
1 thyme sprig
1 rosemary sprig
50ml cabernet sauvignon vinegar
100g redcurrant jelly
300ml brandy
300ml ruby port
300ml red wine
1 litre Chicken Stock (see page 289)
1 litre Veal Stock (see page 289)
100g dark chocolate (75% cocoa solids)

Preheat the oven to 180°C fan. Put the deer bones into a large roasting tray with a little oil and roast in the oven for 30 minutes, until golden brown. Meanwhile, place a large, heavy-based saucepan over a high heat and add a little oil. When the oil is hot, add the deer trimmings to the pan, season with salt and caramelise until well browned. Now add the vegetables, garlic, peppercorns, juniper berries, bay leaf, thyme and rosemary and sweat for 5 minutes, until fragrant. Deglaze the pan with the vinegar, then stir through the jelly. Add the brandy and allow to reduce to a glaze. Next, add the port and allow to reduce to a glaze, then add the red wine and again allow to reduce to a glaze. Add the roasted bones and the stocks and bring to the boil, skimming regularly. Lower the heat and simmer for 1 hour, until reduced to a sauce consistency. Pass through a fine-meshed chinois lined with muslin. Add the chocolate to the finished sauce, stirring until melted, then season with salt if necessary.

Violina Pumpkin Écrasse

1 violina pumpkin
Olive oil
2 garlic cloves, cracked with the blade of a chef's knife
2 thyme sprigs
75ml chardonnay vinegar
75ml extra virgin olive oil

Prepare and light a lidded charcoal barbecue with the defuser plate fitted and maintain a temperature of 150°C. Cut a fifth off the top of the pumpkin, reserving it for the pumpkin discs. Cut the remaining pumpkin in half lengthways and remove all the seeds and stringy pulp. Now score the flesh in a criss-cross pattern and drizzle with a little olive oil. Season with salt, scatter over the garlic and thyme, then place in the barbecue. Pull down the lid and cook for about 2 hours, until the pumpkin is soft, tender and smoky. Scoop the cooked flesh into a bowl and crush using a fork. Stir through the chardonnay vinegar and extra virgin olive oil, and adjust the seasoning, if necessary. Keep warm until needed.

Pumpkin Discs

⅕ pumpkin, reserved from above

Remove the pumpkin skin, then use a mandoline to cut the flesh into slices 2mm thick. Using 2cm and 4cm round cutters, stamp out discs. Wrap them in damp kitchen paper and keep in the fridge until needed.

Brussels Sprout Leaves

16 medium-sized Brussels sprouts

Preheat a deep-fat fryer to 170°C. Using a turning knife, carefully remove the sprout leaves individually, discarding any blemished or pale leaves. Separate the dark ones from the lighter ones. Fry the darker leaves in the deep-fat fryer until they start to colour and stop bubbling. Remove from the fryer, season with salt and drain on kitchen paper. Once drained, transfer to a tray, then place in a dehydrator heated to 70°C and leave for 1 hour to make them extra crispy. Meanwhile, bring a small saucepan of salted water to the boil and blanch the lighter leaves for 10 seconds, before plunging them into iced water. Once cool, drain thoroughly and store in the fridge until needed.

To Finish

Toasted pumpkin seeds
Olive oil
Purple mustard leaves
Green mustard leaves
Mignonette pepper

Warm the Violina Pumpkin Écrasse and
fold through some toasted pumpkin seeds.
Place 2 quenelles of this on a plate, followed
by the Pumpkin Discs glazed with olive oil
and seasoned with salt. Reheat the blanched
Brussels Sprout Leaves, glaze them with
a little oil and arrange them on the pumpkin
together with the crispy Brussels sprout
leaves. Garnish with the purple and green
mustard leaves. Slice the Deer Loins in half,
season with mignonette pepper and place
one half on the plate. Squeeze a generous
dot of the Pontack onto the plate. Warm the
Grand Veneur Sauce and serve on the side.

Côte de Porc, Turnip, Pickled Walnut, Pommery Mustard

Turnips have an interesting bitterness that can be challenging if allowed to overwhelm a dish, but we balance it here with the sweet pork, sharp pickled walnuts and warm Pommery mustard. The pork and turnip ribbons are garnished with freshly ground mignonette pepper, a combination of black and white peppercorns and coriander seeds, for further warmth and a touch of fragrant spice.

Serves 8

Pork Sauce

Vegetable oil
1kg fatty pork trimmings, diced
2 onions, peeled and sliced
2 garlic cloves, cracked with the blade
    of a chef's knife
10 black peppercorns
½ bay leaf
2 thyme sprigs
50ml sherry vinegar
1 litre Chicken Stock (see page 289)
1 litre Veal Stock (see page 289)
Fine sea salt

Place a large, heavy-based saucepan over
a medium–high heat. Once warm, add a little
oil and the pork trimmings. Cook until golden
brown all over and the fat is gently foaming.
Season with salt, then add the onions, garlic,
peppercorns, bay leaf and thyme sprigs and
continue to cook for 2 minutes, until soft.
Deglaze the pan with the sherry vinegar, add
the stocks and bring to the boil, skimming
off any impurities that come to the surface.
Reduce the heat and cook for 45 minutes, until
reduced to a sauce consistency. Pass through
a fine-meshed chinois. Adjust the seasoning,
if necessary, then cool and store until required.

Turnip Purée

500g turnips
50g unsalted butter
300ml Chicken Stock (see page 289)
100g spinach
100g cime di rapa
20g Ultratex

Peel the turnips and slice very finely using
a mandoline. Place a saucepan over a medium
heat. Once warm, add the butter and turnip
slices, then season with salt and sweat for
2 minutes. Add the chicken stock, cover the
pan with a lid and cook for 10 minutes. Remove
the lid, add the spinach and cime di rapa and
cook for a further 2 minutes. Remove the pan
from the heat and transfer to a Vitamix. Add
the Ultratex and blend until smooth. Pass
through a fine-meshed drum sieve and chill
in a bowl over an ice bath.

Turnip Ribbons

2 large turnips

Peel the turnips, then slice into large, thin
sheets using a vegetable sheeter. Cut each
sheet into 20 × 2.5cm strips and store in cold
water until needed.

Côte de Porc

Vegetable oil
4-bone côte de porc (about 1.2kg)
Unsalted butter

Preheat the oven to 200ºC no fan. Season
all sides of the côte de porc with fine sea salt.
Place a large cast-iron frying pan over a high
heat. Once hot, add a little oil and place the
pork in it, fat-side down, until the fat renders
and caramelises. Sear the remaining sides of
the pork for 1 minute each. Add 2 knobs of
butter to the pan and, when foaming, baste
the pork with it for 2 minutes, turning the meat
frequently. Transfer the pork to a wire rack
over a roasting tray and place in the oven for
3 minutes. Turn the pork over and return to the
oven for a further 3 minutes. Leave to rest for
10 minutes before carving it off the bone, then
slice in half lengthways. Trim off any excess fat.

To Finish

Vinaigrette (see page 290)
Baby Tokyo Turnips (see page 127)
Baby turnip leaves
Baby mizuna leaves
Brassica flowers
Pickled Walnut Purée (see page 264)
Pommery mustard
Flaky sea salt
Freshly ground mignonette pepper

Lightly dress and season the Turnip Ribbons
with vinaigrette, salt and mignonette pepper
and roll into cylinders. Warm the baby Tokyo
turnips and dress in vinaigrette. Arrange
the turnip cylinders on a plate with the baby
turnips, dot with the warmed Turnip Purée,
then garnish with the leaves and flowers. Place
the carved Côte de Porc on the plate, season
with a little flaky sea salt and grind mignonette
pepper over the fat. Place a generous dot of
pickled walnut purée next to the pork. Warm
through the Pork Sauce and mix in a little
Pommery mustard to finish. Transfer to a jug
and serve at the table.

Vacherin Mont d'Or, Onion Tarte Fine, Dill Pickles, Mustard

Vacherin Mont d'Or is a seasonal cheese from the Jura region of France and Switzerland that is available only between September and April, so when it arrives in the kitchen at the beginning of autumn, there is a real sense of excitement. In the Jura, they spoon it straight from the rind, but elsewhere they bake it before eating. We make a fondue and serve it with a delicate onion tart, sharp dill pickles and pickled mustard seeds.

Serves 8

White Wine Infusion

200ml white wine
2 garlic cloves cracked
1 rosemary sprig
1 thyme sprig
5 black peppercorns

Put the wine into a container with the garlic, herbs and peppercorns. Leave to infuse in the fridge for at least a week.

Chicken Reduction

500ml Chicken Stock (see page 289)
1 thyme sprig
1 garlic clove, cracked with the blade of a chef's knife
½ bay leaf
5 black peppercorns

Put all the ingredients into a saucepan and place over a medium–high heat. Bring to the boil and reduce the stock by half. This will take roughly 15 minutes. Pass through a fine-meshed chinois and put to one side until required.

Pastry Rings

Flour, for dusting
500g Puff Pastry (see page 290)
50g dextrose powder
50g icing sugar

Preheat the oven to 200°C no fan. On a floured surface, roll out the puff pastry until 4mm thick. Use a round cutter to stamp out 10cm discs. Place on a baking tray lined with baking paper, then cover with a second piece of baking paper and a heavy baking tray. Place in the oven for 10 minutes. Remove from the oven and lower the temperature to 180°C no fan. Use a 9cm round cutter to cut each disc into a neat circle; discard the trimmings. Now use a 5cm round cutter to cut a small central circle in each disc, and discard the middle, leaving a pastry ring. Mix the dextrose powder with the icing sugar, then dust this over the pastry. Place in the oven for 4–6 minutes, until the sugar has melted and the pastry is shiny. Allow to cool, then store until needed.

Lyonnaise Onions

Vegetable oil
4 Spanish onions, peeled and finely sliced
Bouquet garni (2 garlic cloves, 1 bay leaf, 1 thyme sprig, 10 white peppercorns in a bouquet garni bag)
Sherry vinegar
Fine sea salt and freshly ground white pepper

Place a saucepan over a medium heat and add a little oil. When hot, add the onions, season with salt and pepper and sweat until translucent. Add the bouquet garni bag and continue to cook until well caramelised. Remove the bag, then chop the onions by hand. Adjust the seasoning, if necessary, and add sherry vinegar to taste. Put to one side until needed.

Dill Pickle Gel

500ml dill pickling liquid
10g agar agar

Put the dill pickling liquid into a saucepan over a medium heat, whisk in the agar agar and bring to the boil for 2 minutes. Pour into a tray and place in the fridge to set. Once set, transfer the gel to a Vitamix and blend until smooth. Pass through a fine-meshed drum sieve, then pour into a squeezy bottle for service.

Vacherin Fondue

When cheese is heated, particularly when there are multiple cheeses, it has a tendency to split because the milk solids and oil separate as it melts. To stop this happening, we add acid in the form of white wine (tartaric acid) and sodium citrate (citric acid), which act as emulsifying agents.

20g cornflour
250ml Chicken Reduction (see far left)
200g Cheddar, grated
200g aged Gruyère, grated
200g Vacherin Mont d'Or, rind removed
100ml double cream
100ml White Wine Infusion (see top left)
10g sodium citrate
Freshly ground white pepper

Make a slurry by mixing the cornflour with 20ml water. Next, put the chicken reduction into a saucepan, place over a medium heat and bring to the boil. When boiling, add the slurry and bring to the boil again, stirring constantly. When thick, reduce the heat to low and add the cheeses. Whisk over the heat until all the cheeses are incorporated, then add the cream, wine infusion and sodium citrate, and season with fine sea salt and white pepper. Check the seasoning and consistency, and adjust if necessary. Pass through a fine-meshed chinois, allow to cool, then store in the fridge until service.

To Finish

Dill pickles, cut into diamonds
Grilled Baby Onion Petals (see page 96)
Black Garlic Purée (see page 148)
Pickled Mustard Seeds (see page 148)
Mustard frills
Nasturtium leaves
Chervil tips
Chive tips
Purple and white garlic chive flowers

Spoon the Lyonnaise Onions onto the Pastry Rings and top them with dill pickle diamonds and grilled baby onion petals. Next, dot with the Dill Pickle Gel and black garlic purée. Fill 2 of the onion shells with pickled mustard seeds and garnish with the herbs and flowers. Place the dressed rings in the middle of the plates. Gently warm the Vacherin Fondue and pour into the middle of the rings at the table.

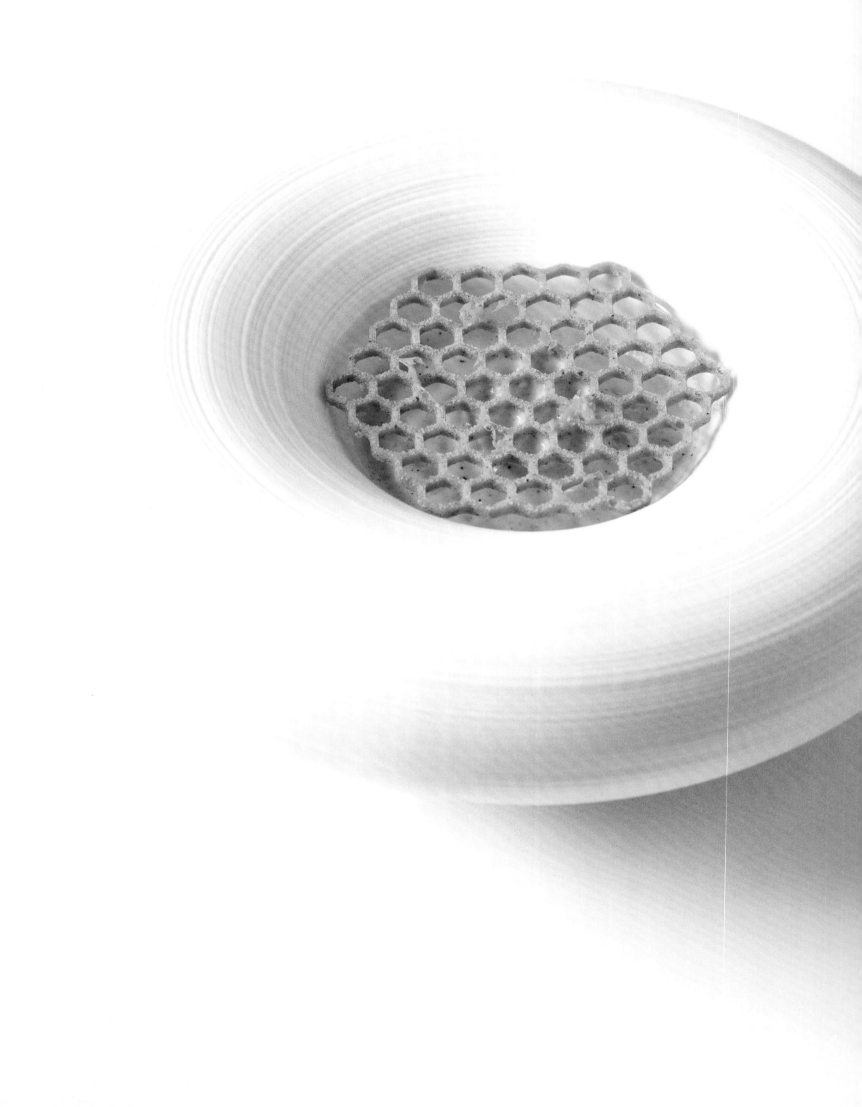

Quince Sorbet, Heather Honey, Pain d'Épices

Quince, pear's sharper and more aromatic cousin, has a distinct flavour and lovely acidity when cooked, but it needs careful handling to get the best out of its tart, unyielding flesh. We poach it for 12 hours with herbs, peppercorns and orange peel, then turn it into an intense but refreshing sorbet and serve it with a gently spiced heather honey mousse and a stunning honeycomb-inspired tuille.

Serves 8

Quince Purée

- 4 quinces
- 300g caster sugar
- 4 rosemary sprigs
- 2 lemon thyme sprigs
- 1 bay leaf
- 2 strips of orange peel
- 10 black peppercorns
- 100ml Stock Syrup (see page 290)
- 50ml quince vinegar
- 5g fine sea salt

Peel, core and quarter the quinces, reserving the skins. Put the sugar into a saucepan with 700ml water and add the rosemary, lemon thyme, bay leaf, orange peel, peppercorns and quince skins. Place the pan over a medium heat and bring to the boil. Set aside to infuse for 20 minutes, then pass through a fine-meshed chinois. Put the quince quarters into a sous-vide bag with the infused liquid and seal under vacuum. Heat a water bath to 95°C and place the bag in it for 12 hours. Strain off and reserve the poaching liquid. Place the quinces, stock syrup, quince vinegar and salt in a Vitamix and blend until smooth, then pass through a fine-meshed drum sieve. Store in the fridge until needed.

Quince Sorbet

- 750g quince purée
- 90ml poaching liquid, reserved from previous step
- 35ml lemon juice
- 65ml quince vinegar
- 35g glucose powder
- 4g super neutrose
- 60g Stock Syrup (see page 290)

Put all the ingredients into a bowl and mix together using a hand-held blender. Pour into Pacojet beakers, then place in the freezer. For service, churn the sorbet in a Pacojet machine.

Heather Honey Mousse

We start by scalding the milk, which means heating it just until it begins to boil, to ensure it's warm enough to take on all the flavours imparted by the honey, spices and zest. Making the custard base with warm scalded milk also allows the sugar to dissolve more quickly and the eggs to cook more gradually, preventing them from curdling.

- 335ml whole milk
- 335ml double cream
- 75g heather honey
- Seeds from ½ vanilla pod
- 2g ground cinnamon
- 2g ground ginger
- 5g orange zest
- 30g sugar
- 120g pasteurised egg yolks
- 5g gelatine leaves, bloomed in cold water

Put the milk, cream, honey, vanilla seeds, spices and zest into a saucepan and place over a medium heat. Bring just to the boil to scald the milk, then remove from the heat. Whisk the sugar and egg yolks together until pale, then add the scalded milk and heat to 84°C, stirring continuously. Add the bloomed gelatine and stir to combine. Pass through a fine-meshed chinois and cool in a bowl over iced water. Once cool, transfer to a siphon charged with 1 nitrous oxide charge and set aside until required.

Pain d'Épices Tuile

- 150g plain flour
- 100g pasteurised egg whites
- 100g dark brown sugar
- 100ml melted butter
- 2g ground cinnamon
- 1g ground nutmeg
- 2g ground ginger

Preheat the oven to 160°C no fan. Mix all the ingredients together until well combined. Spread the mixture into honeycomb moulds and bake for 2 minutes. Turn them around and bake for another 2 minutes. Remove from the moulds and allow to cool. Store in an airtight container until needed.

To Finish

Orange zest

Place a scoop of Quince Sorbet in a bowl and cover with the Heather Honey Mousse. Top with a Pain d'Épices Tuile and garnish with a little fresh orange zest.

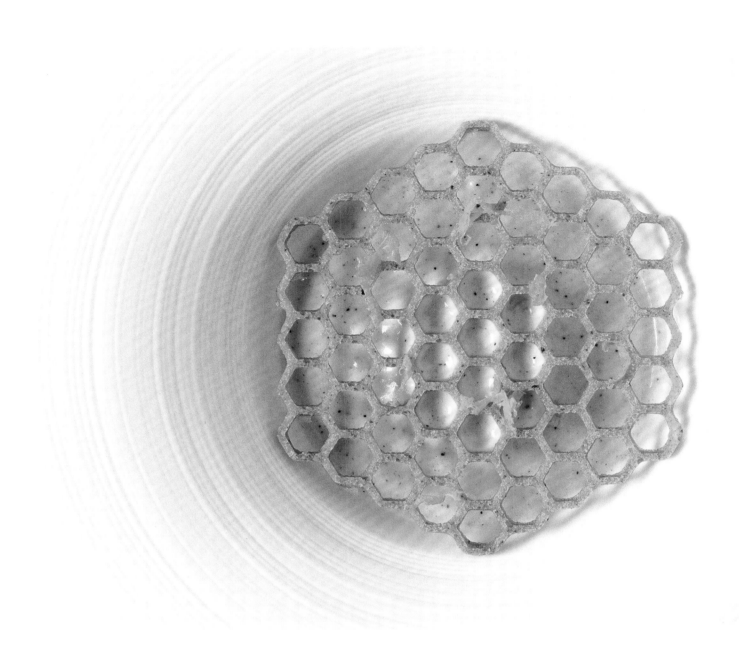

Mont Blanc, Smoked Chestnut, Vanilla, Rum

Our take on this old-fashioned French dessert includes a secret ingredient that makes it highly evocative of autumn; we stir oak-smoked water through the chestnut purée to give it the deeply nostalgic flavour of sweet chestnuts roasting over a wood fire. The Diplomatico rum caramel sauce and gel add an extra warmth that makes this a favourite in the restaurant as the nights draw in and the temperature starts to drop.

Serves 8

Smoked Chestnut Purée

800g cooked chestnuts
2 used vanilla pods
325ml Stock Syrup (see page 290)
5g fine sea salt
50ml oak-smoked water

Put all the ingredients into a saucepan and cover with 750ml water. Place the pan over a medium–high heat and bring to the boil. Reduce the heat and allow to simmer for 1 hour, until the liquid has reduced by half. Remove the vanilla pods, then transfer the mixture to a Vitamix and blend to a smooth purée. Pass through a fine-meshed drum sieve, then set aside until required.

Chestnut Crumble

40g Lescure butter
30g caster sugar
100g chestnut flour
25g toasted buckwheat
2g fine sea salt
1g ground cinnamon
1g ground cloves
20ml whole milk

Preheat the oven to 170°C no fan. Put the butter and sugar into the bowl of a stand mixer and cream them together. Add the chestnut flour, buckwheat, salt and spices, then pour in the milk and mix together until a crumble forms. Spread the mixture over a baking tray lined with a silicone mat and place in the oven for 15–20 minutes, until golden brown. Remove from the oven and allow to cool.

Smoked Chestnut Parfait

115g pasteurised egg yolks
50g caster sugar
375g double cream
2 gelatine leaves, bloomed in cold water
175g Smoked Chestnut Purée, at room temperature (see left)
Chestnut Crumble (see below left)

Put the egg yolks into the bowl of a stand mixer fitted with a whisk attachment and whisk on a medium speed until pale and fluffy. Put the sugar into a small saucepan with 50ml water, then place over a medium–high heat and bring up to 118°C. Slowly drizzle this sugar syrup into the eggs, whisking constantly and being careful to avoid the sides of the bowl. Once the sugar is incorporated, whisk on full speed until the mixture has cooled and become light and fluffy. Put 50ml of the cream into a small saucepan and bring to the boil. Add the bloomed gelatine, stir to dissolve, then add to the eggs along with the Smoked Chestnut Purée. Whisk the remaining cream to soft ribbon stage and gently fold it through the rest of the mix. Transfer the parfait mixture to a piping bag and fill 8 Mont Blanc moulds. Sprinkle Chestnut Crumble over the top to create the base, then place in the freezer for a minimum of 12 hours.

Meringue Straws

100g caster sugar
50g pasteurised egg whites
Seeds from 1 vanilla pod

Preheat the oven to 60°C no fan. Put the sugar and egg whites into the bowl of a stand mixer, then place the bowl over a bain-marie. Using a hand-held whisk, whisk until the sugar has dissolved. Add the vanilla seeds, then put the bowl under the stand mixer and whisk until cold, thick and glossy. Transfer to a piping bag fitted with a 3mm nozzle and pipe in long straight lines onto a baking tray lined with a silicone mat. Place in the oven for 3 hours, until the meringue is crisp. Allow to cool, then cut into straws 5cm long and store in an airtight container until required.

Diplomatico Rum Gel

500ml Diplomatico rum
200ml Stock Syrup (see page 290)
16g agar agar

Put the rum and stock syrup into a saucepan with 100ml water over a medium heat, whisk in the agar agar and bring to the boil for 2 minutes. Pour into a tray and place in the fridge to set. Once set, transfer the gel to a Vitamix and blend until smooth. Pass through a fine-meshed drum sieve, then pour into a squeezy bottle for service.

Chocolate Spray

250g Valrhona Ivoire white chocolate
250g cocoa butter

Melt the chocolate and stir through the cocoa butter. Decant the mixture into a chocolate spray gun. Remove the parfaits from their moulds and spray them all over with chocolate. Return the parfaits to the freezer until service.

Rum Caramel Sauce

25ml Diplomatico rum
250g Caramel Sauce (see page 273)

Stir the rum through the caramel sauce, then transfer to a squeezy bottle for service.

To Finish

Gold leaf

Place a Smoked Chestnut Parfait right of centre on a plate. Decorate with various-sized dots of Diplomatico Rum Gel. Add the Meringue Straws and garnish with the gold leaf. Serve with the warmed Rum Caramel Sauce at the table.

Winter

During the winter, London can look a little drab because the days are short and the sky is often grey. Added to that, it can be bitterly cold, so we find pleasure and comfort in rich, hearty food. It lifts the spirits when we most need it to.

Unlike spring produce, which is bright and light, and summer's, which is vibrant and colourful, winter flavours and colours tend to be earthy and deep. Nonetheless, they offer lots of opportunities for bringing flair and creativity to every dish.

Among the ingredients that shine during winter, root vegetables really stand out. It's easy to turn them into a rich and sustaining dish, but in our kitchen we focus on how to balance that richness by adding an extra dimension, which also helps to bring a touch of lightness, elegance and colour. Playing around with possible combinations changes the conversation about food during the winter and allows us to stay at the forefront of dining too.

Apart from root veg, we love using pumpkin, Jerusalem artichoke, leek, cauliflower and watercress, rhubarb and black truffle, beautiful ingredients that enhance many winter dishes. These are served with spectacular fish and meat, such as Cornish turbot with delica pumpkin écrasse, roast chicken with Jerusalem artichoke, Dover sole with leek purée and truffle, and smoked eel with white onion, caviar and watercress.

Traditionally, winter vegetables have been used to build a heavy, hearty dining experience, but in our kitchen, we approach each one as an opportunity to reveal a new aspect of it and shed light on a quality that guests may not have appreciated before. Winter ingredients in Britain are a somewhat untapped area of exploration, but they can offer just as magical a dining experience as those in any other season.

Inspirational ingredients

Scallops
The cold, clear waters around Scotland are home to excellent scallops, so that's where we get our supplies from – east coast or west coast, depending on the weather. The colder the water, the slower the scallops grow, so the large ones hand-picked by local scallop divers are a prized catch. Hand-diving is a dangerous operation because of the strong currents, but rewarding too, as the scallops fetch a premium price. Once harvested, they are sent to us overnight.

The scallops are large (we generally get three to a kilo) and delivered to us still alive in their shells, which means they are in the absolute best condition. The chefs shuck them for the day's service, then remove the roe and skirt. Amazingly, the remaining scallop meat can weigh up to 120g, which is enough for a main course. By contrast, regular scallops weigh about 25g.

We use the scallop meat raw as a tartare or as sashimi. We also pan-sear whole scallops on one side, glaze them with a little shellfish oil, then finish by grilling them gently over binchotan coal in a Japanese konro grill for five minutes. This allows them to warm through, but they remain barely cooked. The result is a lovely contrast between the caramelised sweetness of the exterior, and the smooth, opaque interior.

As with many of the ingredients in our kitchen, we use every element of the scallop. The fresh roe, and the skirt too, can be diced up and folded through sauces. We also like to dry the roe and shave it over a dish in much the same way that bottarga (dried mullet roe) is used. Sometimes too we grind it to produce a powder that adds an umami punch to a recipe. Finally, the lovely shell is used as a bowl in which to present the finished dish. It is very satisfying that nothing goes to waste.

Jerusalem artichokes
There are several varieties of Jerusalem artichoke tubers, but the type we love to use is called Helianthus, which is less knobbly and a little more cylindrical than the common variety.

When they arrive at the kitchen door, we scrub off any dirt, then place them on baking paper with some thyme, garlic, olive oil, salt and pepper, wrap them up in foil and bake them in the oven. At the start of their season, when they are young and fresh, they cook in about 20 minutes. As the season moves along, the stored tubers become a little firmer, so take longer to cook. Once cooked, we carefully scoop out and season the flesh. True to our policy that nothing goes to waste, the skins are deep-fried to make crisps – absolutely delicious! These are the crowning glory of our roast chicken dish, which is served with crushed Jerusalem artichokes, pickled Chinese artichokes and a black garlic purée. A similar combination works equally well with beef and tender veal sweetbreads.

Jerusalem artichokes make wonderful soups and purées, and in these cases we often keep the skin on because it is full of nutrients, adds an earthy colour and brings depth of flavour too. The tubers can also be used in desserts, such as tarts and ice cream, but here we prefer a white purée, so the peel is removed.

Black Périgord truffle
There is no doubt among our chefs that black Périgord truffle is a highlight of winter eating, and most of our supply comes from producers around Catalonia in Spain. The beauty of black truffle, as opposed to white, is that it's more versatile and doesn't mind being cooked. This makes it useful across a broader range of dishes and ingredients.

When the truffles arrive at the restaurant, they are fairly clean, so we wrap them in kitchen paper, place them in a wooden box and store them in the fridge until needed. Before use, the truffle is scrubbed and dried, then a turning knife is used to peel off the dry outer skin. We freeze those trimmings to tenderise them and then use them to make a purée, dressing or condiment (ground truffle trimmings are mixed with vinegar and olive oil, which we use for a base in dishes such as truffle linguini). We also preserve whole truffles in port, Madeira, brandy and veal stock to extend their season. Nothing is wasted.

Hands down, the chefs' favourite thing to do with black truffles is to add them to scrambled eggs. During the winter, we offer a special in which onion, smoked bacon and truffle ragù are placed in the bottom of a bowl. We then take beautiful eggs from Cornwall, which have rich, saffron-coloured yolks, and gently scramble them in a pan with a little butter, seasoning them only at the very end, off the heat, so as not to draw out their water content. We add a touch of crème fraîche, then place the scrambled eggs on top of the bacon ragù. This is garnished with croutons, chopped chives and dried ham crumbs, then taken out to the dining room, where fresh black truffle is shaved over it in front of the guest.

Black truffle goes with many different things, and in winter lifts some of our favourite dishes. We like to add it to our signature lobster ravioli and grate it over our Dover sole Viennoise. It is also excellent with cheese. We serve a slice of Brie de Meaux with three types of walnut (pickled, candied and toasted) together with shavings of black truffle, then at the table our waiters

drizzle truffle blossom honey over the top. Served with a warm slice of malt bread on the side, this dish is comfort and indulgence on a plate.

Pumpkin
A really versatile vegetable, pumpkin has a gentle sweetness and vibrant colour. Our favourite is the violina pumpkin, which is shaped like a violin case – hence its name – and looks like a long version of butternut squash, but has a thick, rough skin. The colour inside is intense, dark orange, and the seed cavity is relatively small, so you get a lot of flesh to work with. When eaten raw, the flavour is not unlike Charentais melon, a lovely balance of sweetness and acidity, with a floral perfume too.

We prepare violina pumpkin in a fairly simple way: we cut it in half, scoop out the seeds and score it, drizzle the flesh with olive oil, add salt, pepper, thyme and garlic, then place it in a Big Green Egg smoker for about 1½ hours at 150°C. During that time, it develops a nice, smoky flavour. We then scoop out and chop the flesh, season it with salt and pepper, then add olive oil and chardonnay vinegar to bring a bit of sweetness. The flavour is amazing and requires nothing else, though we do sometimes fold in pumpkin seeds for texture.

Smoked violina works beautifully with venison, but more recently we have partnered it with turbot, which is particularly good in the winter. We also serve this lovely fish with compressed raw segments of violina, plus clementine, a citrus purée, shiso leaves and a yuzu citrus beurre blanc. We love using pumpkin and really want to dispel the old-fashioned British notion that pumpkin is usually boringly bland. It's a real hero in our kitchen, and we believe our dishes prove that resoundingly.

Rhubarb
It is really heartening when rhubarb becomes more prevalent in the latter part of winter because it's a sign that the days are slightly warming up. We use forced rhubarb from Yorkshire, the best you can get, which is softer and sweeter than rhubarb harvested during early summer. It is grown in sheds, under the soil, then harvested by candlelight, as even a little daylight will cause photosynthesis, which ruins it. The result of this careful approach is beautiful pink stalks topped with golden leaves. These don't need peeling, but it's a wise precaution with late-season rhubarb to prevent stringiness.

It's a great pity that so many people have grown up with memories of being served only stewed rhubarb, as there are various other possibilities with it. It has a wonderful underlying acidity, so we use it for a number of things across the menu. The sorbet

we make is deliberately sharp so that it can be used as an exclamation mark in a dish, or to create balance against something rich. For instance, we serve it as a dessert with a custard mousse flavoured with fresh vanilla and Sarawak black pepper from Malaysia.

We also like to poach rhubarb. For this, we cut the stalks into batons, vacuum-pack them in a flavoured sugar syrup (one part sugar to one part water) and place them in a water bath at 60°C for 12 minutes. They are then left to cool for 24 hours in the syrup. During this time, the high sugar content of the syrup helps to break down the fibres of the skin, which is partly why we don't have to peel it, and also helps retain the rhubarb's beautiful pink colour. It is served alongside a rice pudding parfait, with stem ginger, lemon balm and orange zest.

Of course, rhubarb works well in savoury dishes too, and it makes a great partner for oily fish, such as mackerel and eel. It also goes really well with game, such as venison, duck and pigeon.

Food often feels like a reward during the winter, when we need more calories to sustain us and keep us warm. While some people may consider the range of ingredients somewhat limited, we believe winter can still offer ample opportunities to make an impact on the plate.

Scallop Sashimi, Shiso, Spring Onion, Shiitake Dashi

Raw scallops and pickled shiitake mushrooms share a similar hard-to-describe texture, and are both rich in umami, the so-called fifth taste that is often described as 'savouriness', which means they complement each other beautifully. The umami levels are boosted further by the shiitake dashi, which contains the umami-rich ingredients kombu seaweed, shio koji fermented rice salt and katsuobushi dried tuna flakes, making this a deeply satisfying dish.

Serves 8

Shiitake Dashi

We use mineral water to make our dashi because the London water that comes out of the tap in the restaurant is too hard. In other words, it has too high a level of calcium, which masks the umami elements of the shiitake, kombu and katsuobushi. By using softer mineral water, we get more flavour in the dashi.

500g fresh shiitake mushrooms, finely sliced
1.5 litres still mineral water
5g kombu
40ml soy sauce
50ml liquid shio koji
2g katsuobushi flakes

Put the sliced mushrooms into a sous-vide bag with the water and seal under vacuum. Heat a water bath to 70°C and place the bag in it for 3 hours. Transfer the bag to the fridge for 24 hours. When the time has elapsed, strain the liquid into a saucepan and discard the mushrooms. Add the kombu, soy sauce and shio koji. Place over a medium heat and bring to 75°C, then remove from the heat and add the katsuobushi flakes. Allow to infuse for 20 minutes, then strain through a fine-meshed sieve and allow to cool.

Pickled Shiitake

We barbecue the shiitake mushrooms before pickling them because cooking them over charcoal boosts their slightly smoky flavour and makes them even tastier.

200g fresh shiitake mushrooms
Vegetable oil
200ml Chicken Stock (see page 289)
150ml dashi vinegar

Light a charcoal barbecue. Remove the stalks from the shiitake mushrooms and lightly wash the caps. Drizzle with a little oil and season with salt. Place on the barbecue and grill for 2 minutes on each side. Transfer the mushrooms to a bowl, bring the chicken stock to the boil and pour it over the mushrooms. Tightly cover the bowl with cling film and leave in a warm place to infuse for 30 minutes. Remove the mushrooms from the stock and cut them lengthways into slices 5mm thick. Cover the sliced mushrooms in the dashi vinegar and set aside until needed.

Scallops

8 extra large scallops

To shuck the scallops, take a knife with a long, narrow blade similar to a boning knife and carefully insert it between the two sides of the shell close to where they join. Keep the blade angled towards the flat shell and make one slice down in a sweeping motion; this will free the flat shell, which can now be discarded. Use the tip of the knife to carefully cut the semi-translucent muscle from between the white scallop meat and the shell – this will free the scallop. Next, carefully slide a thumb between the muscle and the scallop meat to remove the skirt and roe. Wash the scallops gently in iced water and place on kitchen paper until needed.

To Finish

Dashi Vinegar Glaze (see page 119)
Spring onion rings
Purple shiso leaves
Baby nasturtium leaves
Chive flowers
Shiso flowers
Calendula petals

Finely slice each Scallop into about 10 slices from top to bottom. Lightly brush the slices with the dashi vinegar glaze and arrange them in the clean scallop shells in the shape of a flower. Place the Pickled Shiitake between the scallop slices, then garnish with the spring onion rings, the leaves and flowers. Serve with the lightly warmed Shiitake Dashi at the table.

Lobster Ravioli, Black Truffle

A perennial favourite, this dish is never off the menu. The way we serve it has evolved a little since the very early days of the restaurant, but as one of our signature dishes, the ravioli itself stays true to the original recipe – lobster, langoustine and salmon delicately poached in saffron pasta. We change the garnish with each season, but black truffle in winter is the most striking on the plate and the most indulgent to eat.

Serves 8

Lobster Reduction

We roast the lobster heads before starting the stock because it really brings out the sweet shellfish flavours in the bisque for which this reduction is the base. Reducing the stock to a glaze consistency intensifies these flavours even further and gives the bisque its body.

4–6 raw lobster heads
Vegetable oil
1 celery stick
1 large onion, peeled
2 carrots, peeled
½ garlic bulb, peeled and roughly chopped
1½ lemongrass stalks
1 thyme sprig
¼ bay leaf
1 star anise
5 coriander seeds
5 white peppercorns
2 tsp tomato purée
180ml brandy
375ml white wine
1 litre Chicken Stock (see page 289)
1 litre Veal Stock (see page 289)
Fine sea salt

Preheat the oven to 180°C fan. Roughly chop the lobster heads, toss them in a little oil and salt and lay them over a roasting tray. Place in the oven for 20 minutes, until the shells are pink and fragrant. Meanwhile, roughly chop the celery, onion and carrots, then lightly sweat them in a large saucepan with a little oil over a medium heat, until soft. Add the garlic, lemongrass, thyme, bay leaf, star anise, coriander seeds and peppercorns and cook for 1–2 minutes, until aromatic. Add the tomato purée and continue to cook for another minute, then deglaze the pan with the brandy and reduce to a glaze consistency. Once reduced, add the white wine and lobster heads, bring to the boil and reduce by half. Add the stocks, bring back to the boil, then reduce the heat and simmer for 30 minutes. Pass the stock through a fine-meshed chinois. Return it to the pan, bring to the boil, then boil rapidly for 30 minutes, until reduced to a glaze consistency. Pass the stock again, allow to cool and store until needed.

Saffron Pasta

4 whole eggs, plus 6 egg yolks
20ml Saffron Water (see page 290)
550g '00' flour, plus extra for dusting
2g fine sea salt
20ml olive oil

Crack the whole eggs into a bowl, add the extra yolks and the saffron water and whisk thoroughly. Put the flour and salt into a Robot Coupe and, with the machine running, slowly add the olive oil, followed slowly by the eggs, until the mixture resembles breadcrumbs. Test the consistency of the crumb regularly by rubbing a little between your fingers and watching for the dough to begin coming together. At that point, stop adding the egg mixture and reserve it for sticking the ravioli circles together. Bring the dough together by hand and transfer it to a floured surface. Knead for 1–2 minutes, until it begins to show some elasticity, then wrap it tightly in cling film. Place in the fridge to rest for at least 1 hour. Before rolling, remove the pasta dough from the fridge and leave at room temperature for 20–30 minutes. Using a rolling pin, roll the block into a thin sheet on a floured surface before passing it through a pasta machine on the widest setting. Continue passing the sheet through the machine, increasing the setting by 2 each time, until it is halfway down the settings. Fold the ends into the middle and pass the dough through the machine again, open ends first, from the widest setting to the middle setting. Repeat this step 3 more times to work the gluten, then increase the setting and pass the dough through the machine until it is approximately 1–1.5mm thick and you can see your hand through it. Use a 9cm round pastry cutter to stamp out discs, then store them in the fridge until needed.

Salmon Mousse

500g salmon fillet
10g fine sea salt
100ml double cream

Peel the skin from the salmon fillet and remove any bones. Dice the flesh, then place in a cold Robot Coupe with the salt and blend until smooth. Pass the salmon through a fine-meshed drum sieve. Return to the Robot Coupe, add the cream and pulse until you have a smooth, light mousse. Transfer to a container and store in the fridge until needed.

Ravioli Filling

230g diced blanched lobster
   (see preparation, page 119)
65g diced langoustine
65g diced salmon
4g fine sea salt
15ml dashi vinegar
5g chervil, finely chopped
5g chives, finely chopped
10g black truffle, finely chopped
90g Salmon Mousse (see below left)

Place the lobster, langoustine and salmon in a bowl over ice and gently mix together with the salt and dashi vinegar. Add the herbs and black truffle, then fold through the salmon mousse. To check the seasoning, make a small ballotine of the filling wrapped in cling film and poach it in boiling water for 2–3 minutes. Taste, then adjust the seasoning of the remaining filling as required. Weigh the mixture into 65g portions and roll into balls by hand. Store in the fridge until needed.

Black Truffle Purée

As this truffle paste needs to be intensely black to create the dramatic swirl on the white plate, we add vegetable carbon, which is a natural food colouring used mostly in baking. It doesn't add any flavour – we leave that to the fresh truffle and intense truffle juice, which is made by cooking truffles in water during truffle season so the powerful flavour can be used all year round.

250g small black truffle pieces
100ml truffle juice
25ml aged balsamic vinegar
10ml Barolo vinegar
10g vegetable carbon

Put all the ingredients into a Vitamix and blend until smooth. Adjust the seasoning, if necessary, then pass through a fine-meshed drum sieve. Pour into a squeezy bottle and reserve until needed.

Lobster Bisque

125ml Lobster Reduction (see opposite)
375ml whole milk
125ml double cream
25ml brandy
10ml sherry vinegar

Heat the reduction in a saucepan, then whisk in the milk and cream and bring to the boil. Remove the pan from the heat, season with salt and stir through the brandy and sherry vinegar. Adjust the seasoning, if necessary, and keep warm for service.

To Finish

Vinaigrette (see page 290)
Truffle discs

Place a ball of the Ravioli Filling in the middle of each Saffron Pasta disc. Brush around the edge of the discs with any egg and saffron mixture left over from the pasta, or use beaten egg instead. Place a second pasta disc over the filling and pinch between fingers and thumb all around the edge until the ravioli is sealed. Trim with scissors to leave a 1cm border around the filling and create a perfect circle. Repeat this step to make the rest of the ravioli. Bring a pan of salted water to the boil, reduce to a simmer and cook the ravioli for 5 minutes. Lift them out with a slotted spoon and allow to drain. Decorate a plate with a swirl of Black Truffle Purée, then place a ravioli in the centre. Drizzle with a little vinaigrette, then dot the top with a little black truffle purée to secure a truffle disc on each one. Warm the Lobster Bisque, being careful not to boil it, then aerate it with a hand-held milk frother before decanting into a jug. The bisque is poured over the ravioli at the table.

Smoked Eel, White Onion, Caviar, Watercress

To add decadence to smoked eel fillets we coat them in a layer of golden Oscietra caviar, which looks and tastes stunning. The other star of this dish is the humble onion, which we purée and pickle and use to flavour the smoked eel milk foam. Golden crispy shallot rings and allium buds are added at the end to further enhance the onion flavours throughout the dish.

Serves 8

Pickled Smoked Onions

100ml House Pickling Liquor (see page 289)
75ml oak-smoked water
35ml Stock Syrup (see page 290)
20 baby onions, peeled and halved
Fine sea salt

Mix the pickling liquor, smoked water and stock syrup together and season with salt. Pour into a sous-vide bag and add the onions. Seal the bag under vacuum and leave to marinate in the fridge for 48 hours. Once the time has elapsed, heat a water bath to 95°C and place the bag in it for 30 minutes, until the onions are cooked through. Transfer the bag to an ice bath to cool. Once cool, separate the onions into individual petals and store in the cooking liquor until needed.

Onion Purée

1kg onions
100ml double cream
1% Gellan F

Peel and finely slice the onions, place them in a bowl and season with salt. Mix together, then put them into a sous-vide bag and seal under vacuum. Bring a large saucepan of water to the boil, add the bag and boil for 45 minutes, until the onions are tender. Transfer the contents of the bag to a Thermomix, add the cream and blend together. Weigh the purée to calculate 1%, then add this amount of Gellan F to it. Blend together until the temperature reaches 90°C, then pour into a tray and place in a blast chiller to set. Once completely set, return the purée to the Thermomix, blend until smooth and adjust the seasoning, if necessary. Pass through a fine-meshed drum sieve and allow to cool until needed for service.

Smoked Eel

1 whole smoked eel

Peel the skin from the eel by using a thumb to get between the skin and the flesh, starting from the open belly area and peeling towards the top fin; reserve the skin for the sauce. Using a sharp filleting knife, remove the 2 fillets from the eel, reserving the bones but discarding the head. Use fish tweezers to pin-bone the fillets. Turn the fillets over and use the back of the knife to carefully scrape off any excess fat, revealing the light pink flesh underneath. Cut each fillet into 2 large, diamond-shaped pieces, reserving the trimmings and thin tail end for the sauce. Store in the fridge until service.

Eel Milk

2 onions, peeled and finely sliced
1 litre whole milk
Reserved smoked eel trimmings, bones and skin
½ bay leaf
5g coriander seeds

Put all the ingredients into a saucepan, season with a little salt and place over a medium heat. Bring almost to boiling, then reduce the heat and allow to simmer gently for 20 minutes. Pass through a fine-meshed chinois and adjust the seasoning, if necessary. Cool and store until required.

Crispy Shallot Rings

Vegetable oil
5 small banana shallots, peeled
Plain flour

Preheat a deep-fat fryer to 170°C. Using a mandoline, slice the shallots no thicker than 2mm. Separate the shallot rings and select those that are between 1 and 1.5cm in diameter. Coat the rings with a little flour and fry until golden. Season with salt and store in an airtight container for service.

To Finish

Golden Oscietra caviar
Watercress
Allium buds

Preheat the grill. Place the diamond-shaped Smoked Eel pieces under the grill to gently warm through, then cover evenly with the caviar. Place a double swipe of warmed Onion Purée on a plate and sit the eel at an angle on top. Arrange the warmed Pickled Smoked Onion petals beside the eel, and garnish with the Crispy Shallot Rings, watercress and allium buds. Finish at the table with the warmed, aerated Eel Milk.

Dover Sole 'Viennoise', Potato, Leek, Black Truffle, Vin Jaune

Fillets of Dover sole are wrapped around a striking black truffle and scallop mousse, and coated in a Parmesan and truffle crust in our very loose interpretation of a Viennese schnitzel. Linzer potatoes are served alongside with dots of smooth leek purée, just-cooked baby leeks, pickled girolles and thin discs of truffle for colour, crunch and contrast.

Serves 8

Truffle Crust

100g brioche
50g panko breadcrumbs
100g unsalted butter, diced
75g aged Parmesan, finely grated
75g aged Gruyère, finely grated
25g black truffle, finely chopped
Fine sea salt and freshly ground
    black pepper

Preheat the oven to 110°C. Roughly chop the brioche, spread it over a baking tray and place in the oven for 30 minutes, until golden brown and toasted. Allow to cool, then place in a Thermomix and blitz to a crumb. Transfer the brioche crumbs to the bowl of a stand mixer fitted with a paddle attachment and add the panko, butter, Parmesan, Gruyère and truffle. Season with salt and pepper, then slowly mix together until fully combined, being careful not to overmix. Once brought together, roll the mixture between 2 sheets of baking paper until 3mm thick. Place in the freezer to set for 30 minutes. Once frozen, cut into rectangles 18 × 4cm and store in the fridge until required.

Spinach Purée

500g baby spinach leaves
10g Ultratex

Bring a medium-sized saucepan of salted water to the boil. Blanch the spinach for 30 seconds, then plunge into iced water. Once cool, squeeze the leaves dry. Transfer them to a Vitamix, add the Ultratex and blend until smooth. Put the purée into a Pacojet beaker and freeze. Once frozen, churn in the Pacojet machine when required.

Leek Purée

We use only the white parts of the leek for this purée because they have the most delicate flavour. As the flesh gets greener, it becomes more pungent and even slightly bitter, so we use the dark green parts for flavouring stocks and sauces instead.

1kg leeks, white parts only
100ml double cream
50g Spinach Purée (see above), defrosted
1% Gellan F

Finely slice the leeks, put them into a bowl and season with salt. Mix together, then transfer to a sous-vide bag and seal under vacuum. Bring a large saucepan of water to the boil. Put the bag into the pan and boil for 45 minutes, until the leeks are tender. Transfer the contents of the bag to a Thermomix, add the cream and spinach purée and blend together. Weigh the purée, calculate 1% of it, then add this amount of Gellan F to the purée. Blend together until the temperature reaches 90°C, then pour into a tray and place in a blast chiller to set. When completely set, return the purée to the Thermomix, blend until smooth and adjust the seasoning, if necessary. Pass through a fine-meshed drum sieve and cool until needed for service.

Smoked Linzer Potatoes

100g baby Linzer potatoes
50g unsalted butter
5ml oak-smoked water
2g fine sea salt

Wash the potatoes thoroughly, then put them into a sous-vide bag with the butter, smoked water and salt and seal under vacuum. Heat a water bath to 95°C, place the bag in it for 30 minutes, then cool in an ice bath.

Baby Leeks

8 baby leeks

Bring a medium-sized saucepan of salted water to the boil. Trim the root from the leeks, then blanch them in the boiling water for 2 minutes before plunging them into iced water. Once cooled, pat the leeks dry and cut diagonally into 3 equal pieces. Store in the fridge until needed.

Potato Crisps

100g baby Linzer potatoes

Finely slice the potatoes on a mandoline and wash off the excess starch under cold running water. Preheat a deep-fat fryer to 150°C and fry the potato slices until they turn golden brown. Drain them on kitchen paper, then season with salt and store in an airtight container until needed.

Vin Jaune Cream

125g unsalted butter
200g carrots, peeled and grated
50g button mushrooms, sliced
1 garlic clove, cracked with the blade of a chef's knife
1 thyme sprig
¼ bay leaf
500ml vin jaune
500ml Chicken Stock (see page 289)
500ml double cream
100g crème fraîche

Place a saucepan over a medium heat and add the butter. Once melted, add the carrots, mushrooms, garlic, thyme and bay leaf. Season with salt and gently sweat for 10 minutes without colouring. Add the vin jaune and reduce by half. Add the stock and reduce by half. Add the cream and bring to the boil. Reduce the heat and simmer gently for 20 minutes, then pass through a fine-meshed chinois. Using a hand-held blender, mix in the crème fraiche and adjust the seasoning, if necessary.

Scallop and Truffle Mousse

180g scallop meat
60ml double cream
20g Black Truffle Purée (see page 231)
20g black truffle, finely chopped
15g shallot, finely chopped

Place the scallop meat in a cold Robot Coupe, lightly season with salt and blend to a smooth purée. Transfer to a bowl placed over iced water and gently whisk in the cream. Add the remaining ingredients and mix well. To check the seasoning, make a small ballotine of the mousse wrapped in cling film and poach it in boiling water for 3 minutes. Taste, then adjust the seasoning of the remaining mousse, if necessary. Transfer to a piping bag and store in the fridge until needed.

Pickled Girolles

Olive oil
100g girolles
100ml Apricot Gastrique (see page 88)

Place a frying pan over a medium heat and add a little olive oil. When hot, add the girolles and a pinch of salt and sauté gently until the mushrooms have released their moisture, but do not allow them to colour. Cover with the apricot gastrique and bring to a simmer. Gently cook for 1 minute, then remove from the heat. Adjust the seasoning if necessary and store until needed.

Dover Sole

4 × 800g Dover soles
Meat glue
Scallop and Truffle Mousse (see left)
Olive oil

Bring a small saucepan of water to the boil. Carefully dip the sole tails one at a time in the hot water for 10 seconds. Place the fish on a board and, holding the tails firmly, peel the skin off towards the head, being careful not to tear the flesh. Next, use a sharp knife to remove the 4 fillets from each fish. Lay the fillets on the board, skin-side down, and remove the sinew, then trim the fillets so they are all the same size (ideally 18cm long). Place the fillets on a clean tray, skin-side up, and lightly dust them with meat glue and a little salt. Pipe some mousse down the centre of 8 fillets, then place the other fillets on top. Put each portion of fish onto a square of cling film, drizzle with a little olive oil and wrap carefully, keeping the shape as much as possible. Trim off the excess cling film and tuck the sides underneath. Place a portion in a sous-vide bag and seal under vacuum. Repeat this for all the portions. When ready to cook, heat a water bath to 54°C and place the bags in it for 12 minutes. Remove the fish from the bags, unwrap them and place on kitchen paper to rest.

To Finish

Black Truffle Purée (see page 231)
Truffle discs
Purslane
Chickweed
Allium buds
Flaky sea salt

Place a rectangle of Truffle Crust over the poached Dover Sole portions and grill gently for about 3 minutes, or until the crust is golden brown. Trim the ends off the fish at an angle so that it is 12cm in length. Place on a plate, then add the warmed Smoked Linzer Potatoes and Baby Leeks along one side of the fish. Place dots of Leek Purée and black truffle purée in between the vegetables, then garnish with the Potato Crisps, Pickled Girolles, truffle discs, leaves and buds, and sprinkle with flaky sea salt. Serve the warmed Vin Jaune Cream at the table.

THOSE WITH VISION

In 2018 Michelin asked me to give out the awards for the 2019 *Michelin Guide to Great Britain and Ireland* at the BFI Imax theatre in Waterloo, London. As I gazed at the audience, 250 chefs in their white jackets, it was an unexpectedly emotional moment in my career. Brigade after brigade were waiting on the results of the guide to see where their fortunes lay. I had been in their position myself, so to now be handing out stars to them was overwhelming.

My former chef patron Clare Smyth received two Michelin stars that day, as did James Knappett, who'd left us to become head chef at Kitchen Table in Fitzrovia. I also handed out several one-star awards to people who had been with us as commis chefs.

After the event I was sent a photo of all the chefs who'd attended the ceremony, and only then did I realise just how many of them had come through our kitchen. I'd say it was 30–40 per cent of the audience. The extraordinary things they had achieved were amazing and gratifying, a legacy I could only have dreamed of.

That experience made me realise how much Restaurant Gordon Ramsay has achieved. True, we've set the standard for over two decades and given countless guests an evening they will never forget. But perhaps more lastingly, we've nurtured and inspired so many professionals, giving them the foundation and confidence to take the British culinary landscape to new heights. Of course, this didn't happen overnight, which is perhaps why I was taken aback by how many there actually were at the awards ceremony.

I could see exceptional talent in Clare Smyth early on. She showed the tenacity, the dedication and drive, the creative flair that in time would allow her to step out on her own and make her mark. In fact, two years before she actually wanted her own business, I planted the seed of that idea and ensured she got to see and experience things that would help her. I've always thought it important to get aspiring chefs out of the kitchen now and then, to stand alongside me at events, to travel, to attend restaurant openings, and to eat and drink new things. Chefs need broad horizons and must also understand the commercial side of a business. Clare is now taking on the world with her top-class restaurants, Core in London, and Encore in Sydney. I'm thrilled by her success.

Mark Askew, another of my former head chefs, is a thorough Yorkshire lad and an amazing chef. Now a prolific entrepreneur in his own way, he once lived and breathed Restaurant Gordon Ramsay, and was so quick on the uptake. I could show him absolutely anything and he'd replicate it instantly. He didn't say a lot, but he put heart and soul into everything he did, and it was done meticulously. He was my go-to guy when

I wanted to delegate, the perfect pair of hands to entrust with the restaurant.

Marcus Wareing, now one of Britain's finest chefs and restaurateurs, was hugely important to me back in the early days, when we couldn't afford to shut down for holiday periods, such as Christmas. Fortunately, when I did take time out, he would deputise for me and I knew with total confidence that he had all the bases covered. He was absolutely someone I could rely on to do the job properly.

Angela Hartnett too was another thoroughbred, an excellent chef and manager, who commanded the respect of the restaurant team at all times. She was totally dedicated, and I knew, if need be, she would come in at the drop of a hat and nail whatever task she was given. I can't stress enough how marvellous it is to have had people like her and the others I've mentioned in the kitchen.

From the get-go, my current chef patron, Matt Abé, had all the necessary qualities to run the restaurant. He's now been with us for over 15 years and proved he is an extraordinary chef, respecting the integrity of ingredients, understanding the power of their flavours, and lifting them with flair and restraint. Everything he puts on the plate makes sense and remains true to the principles of the restaurant. He has managed brilliantly to maintain the standards and run the business, while evolving as a chef and putting his own imprint on our dishes.

Matt's biggest challenge now lies ahead of him. Over the next three years we'll put a plan together with him to strike out as an independent and switch on his own restaurant lights. We're already in discussions about this, and I know he will be amazing. In the meantime, we're lining up Kim Ratcharoen to replace Matt, and the process of nurturing and mentoring will begin all over again.

Of course, fine food is just one thing a top restaurant excels at. The other is delivering the very best hospitality and service. Both are genuine art forms, and the dining experience would be vastly inferior without them. I have to mention a few who have made a significant contribution over many years.

James Lloyd, who started as a young commis sommelier in 2002, the year after we first received three Michelin stars, moved up the ranks fast and even spent time with our restaurant group in New York because he is so good. On leaving there, he travelled widely to find his own jewels of the wine world, then returned to Restaurant Gordon Ramsay in 2016 as head sommelier. Devoid of ego, intimidation and stuffiness, he embraces the pleasure of a £32 bottle from the cellar as much as one costing £3000. He can find the joy and purpose in both, thus ensuring that guests feel good about their choice too.

Jean-Claude Breton, who has only recently retired, was the ultimate maître d', the head of our front-of-house staff, who was as much the heart of Restaurant Gordon Ramsay as

I was at the time. Every inch the professional, he embodied the skill of his craft, making guests feel welcome, comfortable and, above all, special. He had the extraordinary ability to remember the names of returning customers and also what they had eaten on their last visit, even if that was two years previously.

For most people, walking into a three-Michelin-star restaurant is quite intimidating because it's a rare, maybe one-off, experience, the treat of their lives. Jean-Claude knew exactly how to put people at their ease, and he demonstrated that beautifully with my mum. She'd be confused about which knife and fork to use, ask questions, such as what's this flat spoon for? Can I get my lamb well done? He dealt with her kindly, in a completely non-patronising way, and she really enjoyed herself.

Another aspect of Jean-Claude, and rarely seen among fellow maître d's, was that he connected with the chefs and really understood the dishes, delivering them to the guests with as much passion and excitement as the people who made them. He always appeared to move effortlessly between dining room and kitchen, where he had to deal with the hot-headed version of me, but he somehow remained unruffled and always kept a smile on his face.

He and I recently celebrated 29 years together because we met five years before Restaurant Gordon Ramsay opened, working first in France and then at Aubergine. I knew how special he was, so when he first moved to London and didn't know anyone, I used to take him out to dinner with Tana. It became so customary that she often said, 'Bloody hell, it's the three of us again! Not much of a date night!'

I think Jean-Claude understood me very early on. He had the measure of my determination, grasped the mission I was on, and wanted to be part of that. His insight meant that he could understand why the ride was sometimes bumpy, and he was willing to put up with the turbulence. In return, I valued his commitment and loyalty, and my respect and admiration for him grew with each passing day. Since retiring, he has become an ambassador for Gordon Ramsay Restaurants, his task being to impart knowledge and to inspire and help nurture the next generation of front-of-house professionals throughout our group. It's an honour to have him in that role.

Given my feelings about Jean-Claude, it will come as no surprise that I was very upset when the food critic A. A. Gill came to dinner and was childishly rude to him. That was too much, and I ended up refusing him entry. Unfortunately, he had two other people with him, one of them a well-known celebrity, but I had to make a stand. I can take people being rude about me and the restaurant, but to take a pop at Jean-Claude ... well, I wasn't standing for that. Gill and I made up a few years later, but I'd had to make it clear the restaurant works as a team. I look after those who look after me. They deserve it. We keep each other's back. That's what we do in restaurants.

The proof, if any were needed, of how well a team delivers to guests is not in the dining room or in the kitchen. I tell people that if they want to assess the success of a restaurant, they should keep an eye on the plates returning to the dishwasher. If those plates are coming back clean, it's clear that every single person in the restaurant is doing their job properly.

There are so many people who have been, and continue to be, part of the success of the restaurant. It's impossible to list them all, but they know who they are, and without them, the restaurant would not be what it is – one team, one dream.

Cornish Turbot, Delica Pumpkin, Clementine, Shiso

Blackened with nori seaweed, two perfectly cooked pieces of turbot sit alongside a bright orange garnish of pumpkin discs and clementine segments, a bold combination that is as vibrant to look at as it is to eat. The dish is served with a citrus beurre blanc flavoured with orange, grapefruit, lemon, yuzu and calamansi (Philippine lime) for a sharp but buttery finish.

Serves 8

Clementine Segments

    250g clementine segments
    5g Pectinex Ultra SP-L
    100ml clementine juice

Put the clementine segments into a sous-vide bag with the Pectinex and 250ml water and seal under vacuum. Place the bag in the fridge for 12 hours. When the time has elapsed, wash the segments in a bowl of cold water and remove any remaining pith. Store the segments in the clementine juice until needed.

Herb Oil

    2 garlic bulbs
    1 litre grapeseed oil
    50g marjoram
    25g rosemary
    25g thyme
    50g basil
    2 bay leaves

Cut the garlic bulbs in half horizontally and put them into a deep-sided saucepan with a little of the oil. Place the pan over a low–medium heat and gently caramelise for 10 minutes, until lightly coloured and aromatic. Once coloured, add the remaining oil and heat to 70°C, then add all the herbs. Remove the pan from the heat and allow to infuse in a warm place for 1 hour. Pass through a fine-meshed chinois and put to one side until needed.

Delica Pumpkin Écrasse

    1 delica pumpkin
    2 garlic cloves, cracked with the blade
        of a chef's knife
    2 thyme sprigs
    20ml calamansi vinegar
    Olive oil
    Fine sea salt

Preheat the oven to 150°C fan. Cut the pumpkin in half and scoop out the seeds and stringy pulp. Season with salt and place a garlic clove and thyme sprig in each half. Wrap tightly in foil and bake for 2 hours, until soft and tender. Scoop out the cooked flesh and finely chop by hand. Season with the calamansi vinegar, a drizzle of olive oil and salt. Store in the fridge until needed.

Clementine Gel

    500g Boiron clementine purée
    Zest of 1 clementine
    10g agar agar

Put the clementine purée and zest into a small saucepan over a medium heat, whisk in the agar agar and bring to the boil for 2 minutes. Pass through a fine-meshed chinois, then pour into a tray and place in the fridge to set. Transfer the gel to a Vitamix and blend until smooth. Pass through a fine-meshed drum sieve, then pour into a squeezy bottle for service.

Nori Powder

The sheets of nori are grilled to make sure they are completely dry and crisp before being blitzed. Nori absorbs moisture from the atmosphere very easily, and an even slightly damp sheet won't break down into the powder we are looking for.

    10 nori sheets
    10g vegetable carbon

Preheat the grill to high. Put the nori sheets onto a baking tray and place under the grill for 1 minute, then turn over for another minute. Put the nori sheets into a Vitamix with the vegetable carbon and blend to a powder. Transfer to an icing duster and set aside until needed.

Turbot

    200g fine sea salt
    8 × 120g portions from a 5–6kg turbot
    Olive oil
    Herb Oil (see left)

Dissolve the salt in 2 litres of water to make a 10% brine. Place the turbot portions in the brine for 10 minutes, then dry thoroughly on kitchen paper. Place each portion of fish in a small sous-vide bag with a drizzle of olive oil and seal under vacuum. Heat a water bath to 54°C and place the bags in it for 8 minutes. Pour the herb oil into a high-sided sauté pan and warm to 65°C. Remove the fish from the bags and place in the oil to confit for 5 minutes to complete the cooking process.

Citrus Beurre Blanc

    500ml grapefruit juice
    500ml lemon juice
    500ml orange juice
    250g unsalted butter, diced
    20ml double cream
    5ml calamansi vinegar
    5ml yuzu juice
    15ml Stock Syrup (see page 290)

Pour the citrus juices into a saucepan over a medium–high heat and reduce to a loose syrup consistency. Before service, pour 50ml of the reduction into a saucepan and place over a medium heat. Add the butter, a little at a time, whisking continuously to emulsify. Finish with the cream, calamansi vinegar, yuzu juice and stock syrup and season with salt. Keep warm for service.

To Finish

    Pumpkin Discs (see page 200)
    Ruby mustard leaves
    Mizuna leaves
    Shiso leaves

Cut the Turbot portions in half and dust well with the Nori Powder. Place 2 pieces of the fish on a plate, then add 2 quenelles of warmed Delica Pumpkin Écrasse next to them. Place 5 Clementine Segments and the pumpkin discs on top of the pumpkin. Next, add dots of Clementine Gel and garnish with the leaves. Serve the warmed Citrus Beurre Blanc at the table.

Roast Chicken, Jerusalem Artichoke, Black Garlic, Jus Gras

While roast chicken is a classic, we take it to the next level by brining the meat, then gently forcing a deliciously light chicken, bacon and thyme mousse under the skin before slow-cooking and roasting the crown. The result is incredibly moist and flavourful meat with crisp, golden skin. Crushed Jerusalem artichokes with deep-fried skins and pickled Chinese artichokes are served on the side, with dots of black garlic purée and seasonal flowers and leaves on top.

Pickled Crosnes

> 200g crosnes (Chinese artichokes)
> 25g fine sea salt
> 300ml House Pickling Liquor (see page 289)

Wash the crosnes thoroughly. Make a 5% brine by dissolving the salt in 500ml water. Put the crosnes into the brine and leave in the fridge for 24 hours. Drain off the brine, then put the crosnes into a medium saucepan. Cover with the pickling liquor and bring to the boil. Leave to simmer for a few minutes, until cooked (this may take longer if the crosnes are large). Drain and adjust the seasoning, if necessary. Allow to cool, then set aside for service.

Dried Celeriac

> 1 large celeriac

Wash and peel the celeriac, then coarsely grate it using a box grater. Spread the flesh over a tray lined with kitchen paper, then place in a dehydrator heated to 75°C and leave for 12 hours. Store in an airtight container until needed.

Chicken, Bacon and Thyme Mousse

> 100g Alsace bacon, finely diced
> 2 skinless chicken breasts
> 50ml double cream
> 50ml vin jaune
> 25ml brandy
> 2 shallots, peeled and finely chopped
> 20g picked thyme leaves
> Fine sea salt and freshly ground
>   black pepper

Place a small frying pan over a medium heat and add the bacon. Sauté for 3 minutes, until just starting to colour. Transfer to kitchen paper to blot up any excess fat, and leave to cool. Next, remove the skin and any sinews from the chicken breasts and dice the flesh into small cubes. Place in a blast chiller for 5 minutes, then blend in a Robot Coupe until smooth. Pass the puréed chicken through a coarse-meshed drum sieve, then place in a bowl, season with salt and black pepper and beat in the double cream. Stir in the wine and brandy, then add the chopped shallots, chopped bacon and thyme leaves and mix well. To check the seasoning, make a small ballotine of the filling wrapped in cling film and poach it in boiling water for 3 minutes. Taste, then adjust the seasoning of the remaining mousse as required. Put the mousse into a piping bag and store in the fridge until needed.

Chicken Preparation

2 × 2kg free-range chickens
400g fine sea salt
Chicken, Bacon and Thyme Mousse
    (see opposite)

Discard the offal and wishbone from both birds, then cut the wings off and reserve them for the jus gras (right). Make a 10% brine by dissolving the salt in 4 litres water. Add the chickens to the brine and leave in the fridge for 1 hour. Drain thoroughly, then turn each chicken over and make an incision down the back. French-trim the leg knuckles, then insert a thumb into the incision and carefully loosen the skin from the legs. Carefully remove the leg through the hole in the skin made when trimming, but leave the skin attached to the chicken. Using scissors, cut off the backbone, leaving the crown and a lot of excess skin. Turn the chicken over and use your fingers to carefully free the skin from the breasts. Pipe the chicken, bacon and thyme mousse under the skin and ensure it is evenly spread across the breasts. Wrap the excess skin around the crown, then wrap the crown tightly in cling film and tie at the ends, removing as much air as possible. Heat a water bath to 65° and place the crown in it for 1 hour. Once cooked, chill in an ice bath for 1 hour. When the time has elapsed, remove the cling film and dry the crown with kitchen paper. Store uncovered in the fridge until required.

Jus Gras

We finish sauces with a little vinegar to cut through the richness and to enhance the flavours in the same way we might add lemon or lime juice. Seasoning isn't just about adding salt and pepper.

Vegetable oil
1.5kg chicken wings, chopped in half
50g unsalted butter
3 shallots, peeled and sliced
100g large button mushrooms, sliced
100g shiitake mushrooms, sliced
3 garlic cloves, cracked with the blade
    of a chef's knife
25g thyme sprigs
50g dried ceps
1 litre Chicken Stock (see page 289)
1 litre Veal Stock (see page 289)
10 white peppercorns
½ bay leaf
100g Dried Celeriac (see opposite)
Sherry vinegar, to taste

Place a heavy-based saucepan over a high heat and add a little oil. When hot, brown the chicken wings in batches, until well coloured all over, and set them aside. Drain off any excess fat after each batch. Once all the chicken wings are cooked, put the butter into the empty pan and, when it is foaming, add the sliced shallots, button and shiitake mushrooms, garlic, thyme and dried ceps. Sweat for 5 minutes, until soft, then return the chicken wings to the pan, season with salt and cover with the chicken and veal stocks. Add the white peppercorns and bay leaf and bring to the boil, skimming off any impurities and excess fat from the surface. Allow the sauce to simmer over a gentle heat for 1 hour, until reduced to a sauce consistency. Remove the pan from the heat, then stir through the dried celeriac and leave to infuse for 20 minutes. Pass the sauce through a fine-meshed chinois, using the back of a ladle to press all the chicken juices from the wings. Adjust the seasoning, if necessary, and add a splash of sherry vinegar to taste. Chill and store in the fridge until needed.

Jerusalem Artichoke Écrasse

1kg Jerusalem artichokes
Olive oil
2 garlic cloves, peeled and crushed
2 thyme sprigs

Preheat the oven to 180°C fan. Wash the artichokes thoroughly, then place in the centre of a large piece of baking paper and coat generously with the oil, crushed garlic, thyme and salt. Wrap the artichokes in the paper, then wrap the parcel tightly in a double layer of foil. Place in the oven for 45 minutes, until tender. Once cooked, cut the artichokes in half and scoop out the flesh, reserving the skins for deep-frying. Chop the flesh finely by hand and adjust the seasoning, if necessary. Place in the fridge until needed.

Jerusalem Artichoke Crisps

Jerusalem artichoke skins, reserved from
    previous step

Preheat a deep-fat fryer to 180°C. Put the reserved artichoke skins into the fryer and fry until golden brown. Season with salt and store in an airtight container until required.

Roasting the Chicken

2 Chicken crowns, reserved from
    preparation step
Vegetable oil

Preheat the oven to 200°C fan. Brush the chicken crown with oil, season with salt, then place on a rack over a roasting tray and put into the oven for 7 minutes. Turn the crown around and cook for a further 7 minutes, then set aside to rest for 15 minutes before carving.

To Finish

Black Garlic Purée (see page 148)
Purslane
Golden thyme
White garlic flowers

Warm the Jerusalem Artichoke Écrasse and place a layer in an oval pastry cutter on a plate. Add some Pickled Crosnes and dot with black garlic purée. Place some Jerusalem Artichoke Crisps on the top, dot with more purée, and garnish with the leaves and flowers. Remove the Chicken breasts from the crown and carve each breast into 2 diamond shapes, discarding the ends. Place on the plate and serve the warmed Jus Gras at the table.

Veal Sweetbread, Toasted Grains, Ajo Blanco, Malt

The mild taste and velvety texture of veal sweetbreads make them an excellent vehicle for many different flavours. Here we glaze them in honey and soy, and serve them with a pair of contrasting sauces – a deep, sweet malt gravy and a garlicky ajo blanco. A combination of puffed wild rice and amaranth seeds with crisp sobacha and malted oats adds a toasted flavour and creates a textural contrast to the soft veal sweetbread hidden within.

Serves 8

Malt Jus

Vegetable oil
1kg veal trimmings
4 shallots, peeled and sliced
2 garlic cloves, peeled and crushed
10 black peppercorns
1 thyme sprig
½ bay leaf
200g malt extract
1 litre Veal Stock (see page 289)
1 litre Chicken Stock (see page 289)
Sherry vinegar, to taste
Fine sea salt

Put a large, heavy-based saucepan over a high heat and, when hot, add some oil. Add the veal trimmings and cook until browned all over. Once browned, add the sliced shallots and crushed garlic and allow to sweat until soft. When soft, add the peppercorns, thyme and bay leaf and continue to cook until aromatic. Next, add the malt extract and stocks and bring to the boil, skimming regularly to remove any impurities that rise to the surface. Reduce the heat and simmer to a sauce consistency. When reduced, pass through a fine-meshed chinois and season with salt and sherry vinegar. Cool and place in the fridge until needed.

Puffed Wild Rice

300ml vegetable oil
100g wild rice

Pour the oil into a medium-sized, high-sided saucepan and place over a high heat. Once the oil has reached 200°C, add the rice, which will puff up in about 5 seconds. Remove the puffed rice from the oil and season with salt. Drain on a tray lined with kitchen paper. Once cool, transfer to an airtight container and set aside.

Puffed Amaranth

50g amaranth seeds

Place a small saucepan over a medium–high heat. When hot, add the seeds and cover with a lid. Keep the seeds moving gently over the heat for 30 seconds, until puffed up. Allow to cool, then store in an airtight container until required.

Sweetbreads

2kg veal heart sweetbreads
Vegetable oil
Unsalted butter

Using a sharp knife, carefully remove the outer membrane from the sweetbreads, discarding any large pieces of fat. Portion the sweetbreads into 100g pieces, place in a container and add just enough vegetable oil to cover. When ready to cook, place a cast-iron frying pan over a high heat. Once hot, add a little oil to the pan and lightly season the sweetbreads with salt. Add them to the pan and fry for 5 minutes, until golden brown. Turn over and cook for another 5 minutes. Add a little butter, allowing it to foam, then baste the sweetbreads with it for 1 minute. Remove from the pan and rest for 5 minutes.

To Finish

Honey Glaze (see page 127)
Sobacha
Malted oats
Allium buds and flowers
Ajo Blanco (see page 67)
Flaky sea salt and freshly ground
    mignonette pepper

Warm some honey glaze in a small saucepan and roll the cooked Sweetbreads in it until nicely glazed. Coat the sweetbreads in the Puffed Wild Rice, Puffed Amaranth, sobacha and malted oats, and season with flaky sea salt and mignonette pepper. Place the sweetbreads on a plate and garnish with the allium buds and flowers. Warm the ajo blanco and carefully pour onto the plate so that it stays on one side of the sweetbreads. Warm the Malt Jus and pour it around the other side of the sweetbreads at the table.

Brie de Meaux, Pickled Walnut, Black Truffle, Malt Loaf

A slice of perfectly ripe Brie de Meaux needs hardly any embellishment, but we can't resist adding an indulgent combination of black truffle shavings, pickled walnut gel and crunchy candied walnut pieces, then drizzling a little truffle honey over the top. This takes a really great ingredient and turns it into something truly sensational.

Serves 8

Truffle Honey

50g black truffle
500g blossom honey

Finely chop the truffle, then cover it with the honey and leave to infuse for 3 days before using.

Malt Loaf

600g dried mixed fruit
300ml freshly brewed English breakfast tea
500g T45 flour
1 tsp bicarbonate of soda
2 tsp baking powder
4 eggs
350g malt extract
170g soft brown sugar

Soak the dried fruit in the hot tea for 1 hour. Preheat the oven to 165°C fan. Line 8 mini loaf tins (10 × 6cm) with baking paper. Sift the flour, bicarbonate of soda and baking powder into a large bowl. Add the eggs and stir together by hand until fully incorporated. Add the malt extract and soft brown sugar, mix until thoroughly combined, then fold through the soaked fruit and any liquid that hasn't been absorbed. Pour the mixture into the lined loaf tins and bake in the oven for 25 minutes. Check whether it is cooked by inserting a metal skewer into the middle of the loaf; if it comes out clean, it is ready. If not, return to the oven for 5 minutes and check again until fully cooked.

Pickled Walnut Purée

780g pickled walnuts, plus their pickling liquor
Fine sea salt

Place the walnuts and pickling liquor in a small saucepan over a medium–high heat. Bring to the boil, reduce the heat and leave to simmer gently for 10 minutes. When the walnuts are soft, allow to cool slightly, then transfer to a Vitamix. Blend until silky smooth and season with salt. Pass the purée through a fine-meshed drum sieve and allow to cool. Transfer to a squeezy bottle for service.

Candied Walnuts

200g caster sugar
200g walnuts

Preheat the oven to 170°C fan. Put the sugar and walnuts into a small saucepan with 250ml water and bring to the boil for 8 minutes. Drain the walnuts through a fine-meshed chinois, then place them on a baking tray lined with a silicone mat and bake for 6 minutes. When ready, set aside to cool to room temperature, and store in an airtight container until required.

To Finish

Brie de Meaux slices
Peeled black truffle
Walnuts

Place a slice of Brie on a plate and allow to come to room temperature. Preheat a grill. Take each Malt Loaf and carefully cut off the crusts at either end. Cut each loaf into 3 slices and toast them under the grill until golden brown. Place dots of the Pickled Walnut Purée and pieces of Candied Walnut on the cheese. Using a Microplane, shave over a generous amount of the truffle and walnuts. Serve with the warmed Malt Loaf on the side and drizzle the cheese with plenty of Truffle Honey at the table.

Rhubarb and Custard

Forced rhubarb arrives in the kitchen in late December, a gorgeous pink beacon in the depths of winter. As it is so delicious in its own right, we make a very simple sorbet and serve it with rhubarb's classic accompaniment, vanilla custard, but reimagined as a very light, melt-in the-mouth mousse. A sprinkling of Sarawak pepper just before serving adds a surprising aromatic warmth that works beautifully with the tang of the rhubarb and creaminess of the custard.

Serves 8

Rhubarb Sorbet

150g caster sugar
500g forced rhubarb, diced

Put the sugar into a saucepan with 100ml
water and place over a medium–high heat.
Bring to the boil, then set aside to cool. Put
the rhubarb into a sous-vide bag with the
cooled syrup and seal under vacuum. Heat
a water bath to 65°C and place the bag in it
for 20 minutes. Transfer the hot rhubarb and
syrup to a Vitamix and blend together, then
pass through a fine-meshed chinois. Pour
into Pacojet beakers and place in the freezer.
Churn in the Pacojet machine when required.

Red Butterfly Tuile

150g plain flour
100g pasteurised egg whites
100g caster sugar
5g fine sea salt
100ml unsalted butter, melted
4g brilliant red powdered food colouring

Preheat the oven to 160°C fan. Mix all the
ingredients together until well combined.
Spread the mixture into butterfly moulds and
bake for 2 minutes. Turn them around and bake
for another 2 minutes. Remove the tuiles from
the moulds and allow to cool.

Vanilla Mousse

340ml whole milk
340ml double cream
Seeds from 1 vanilla pod
30g sugar
120g pasteurised egg yolks
5g bronze gelatine leaves, bloomed
   in cold water

Put the milk, cream and vanilla seeds into
a saucepan over a medium heat. Bring up to
83°C to scald the milk, then remove from the
heat. Whisk the sugar and egg yolks together
until pale, then add the scalded milk and heat
to 84°C. Add the bloomed gelatine and stir to
combine. Pass through a fine-meshed chinois
and cool in a bowl over iced water. Once cool,
transfer to a siphon charged with 2 nitrous
oxide charges and set aside until required.

To Finish

Freshly ground Sarawak pepper

Place a large scoop of Rhubarb Sorbet in a
presentation bowl, then cover with the Vanilla
Mousse and sprinkle with a little Sarawak
pepper. Place a Red Butterfly Tuille on top
before serving.

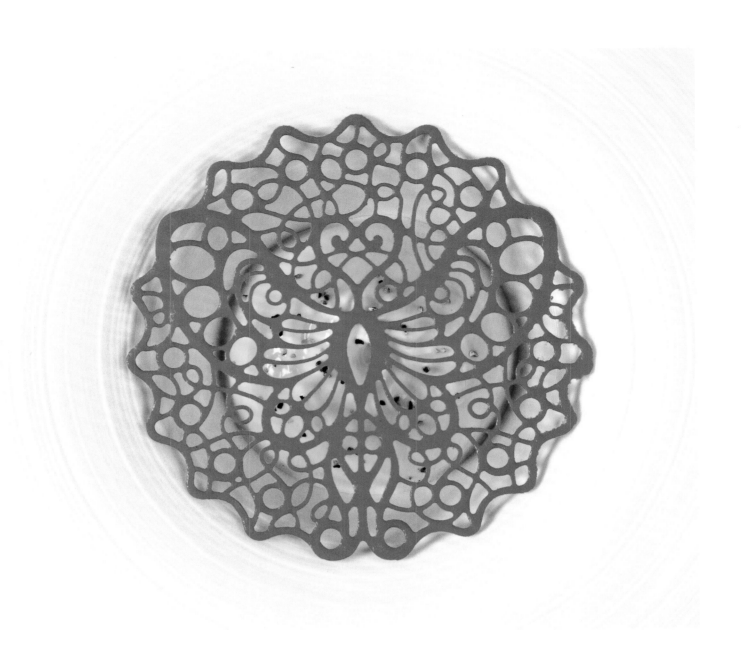

Apple Tarte Tatin, Tahitian Vanilla Ice Cream

Tarte Tatin has been on the menu since the restaurant opened and, indeed, on the menu at Aubergine before that. People expect it to be made with unexpected fruits and unusual flavours, or deconstructed in some way, but we don't mess with the classics. Apples, caramel and puff pastry cooked in traditional copper Tatin pans and served with vanilla ice cream – perfection!

Serves 8

Caramel Sauce

500g caster sugar
700ml double cream

Make a dry caramel by placing the sugar in a medium-sized saucepan over a high heat and allowing it to caramelise until quite dark. Add 500ml of the double cream to the pan and stir to combine, being careful as it will bubble vigorously. Remove the pan from the heat and add the remaining cream. Pass the caramel through a fine-meshed chinois into a container and allow to cool.

Vanilla Ice Cream

1 litre whole milk
325ml double cream
2 Tahitian vanilla pods
270g pasteurised egg yolks
155g caster sugar

Put the milk, cream and vanilla pods into a saucepan, place over a medium–high heat and bring just to the boil. Meanwhile, whisk the egg yolks and sugar together until fully combined, then pour in a little of the scalded liquid to temper the eggs. Mix together, then pour the eggs into the milk pan, stirring continuously, and cook the resulting crème anglaise to 84°C. Remove from the heat, then pass through a fine-meshed chinois into a bowl and cool over ice. When cool, transfer to Pacojet beakers and freeze. Once frozen, churn in the Pacojet machine when required.

Tarte Tatin

200g unsalted butter
200g caster sugar
10 Pink Lady apples, peeled, cored
    and quartered
300g Puff Pastry (see page 290)
Flour, for dusting

Spread 50g of the butter over the bottom of 4 copper sauté pans (16cm in diameter), then cover each with 50g of the sugar. Arrange the apple quarters in the pans, standing 8 pieces, peeled-side down, around the perimeter, and 2 in the middle. Roll out the puff pastry on a lightly floured surface until it is 3–4mm thick. Cut out 4 circles 16cm in diameter and place them over the apples. Carefully tuck the pastry edges down the side of the apples, then place the pans in the fridge for 20 minutes. Preheat the oven to 180°C fan. When the tarts have rested, place the pans over a high heat for about 2 minutes, until the sugar and butter combine into a light brown caramel. Put the pans into the oven and bake for 45–60 minutes, until the pastry is golden brown and crisp. Set aside to cool for 15 minutes before serving.

To Finish

Turn out the Tartes Tatin and cut them in half, placing half a tart on each plate. Serve with a rocher of Vanilla Ice Cream and some warmed Caramel Sauce at the table.

Petit Fours

Just when you think you can't possibly eat another mouthful, a plate of the most delectable chocolates, miniature cakes and tempting jellies arrives at the table with your coffee and after-dinner drinks ... Petits fours are the final chance for our chefs to impress with their creativity and skill, and to send our guests home with a wonderful taste in their mouths. Although these little gems appear conventional, they often have a surprising twist or unexpected ingredient that makes them a bit more interesting than an after-dinner mint. From the very first canapé to the final petit four, eating at Restaurant Gordon Ramsay is an incredible gastronomic journey.

Selection of Petit Fours (overleaf)

Chocolate Crunch
Pistachio and Smoked Salt
Macadamia Nut and Coffee
Peanut
Sobacha

Cakes and Tartlets
Pain d'Épices with Orange Marmalade
Lemon Drizzle
Millionaire Shortbread

Jellies
Raspberry with Verbena Sugar
Calamansi with Sarawak Pepper Sugar
Blackcurrant with Sweet and Sour Sugar

Page 280 (clockwise from top left)
Pistachio and Smoked Salt Chocolate Crunch
Pain d'Épices with Orange Marmalade
Calamansi Jelly in Sarawak Pepper Sugar

Page 281 (clockwise from top left)
Macadamia Nut and Coffee Chocolate Crunch
Lemon Drizzle Cake
Raspberry Jelly in Verbena Sugar

Page 282 (clockwise from top left)
Peanut Chocolate Crunch
Millionaire Shortbread
Blackcurrant Jelly in Sweet and Sour Sugar

The Future

When I was nine years old, I was living with my family in a tiny two-bedroom council flat in Birmingham. We didn't have much. In fact, we barely had anything, and we weren't there long because my dad was caught fiddling the gas meter. He'd worked out a way to get past the seal without breaking it so he could drop a 50p coin in and get the gas running, but the coin would drop out the bottom to be used time and time again. Soon enough he got busted and we had to move on.

Before that happened, though, we'd had a great relationship with our Pakistani landlord, a lovely man with a long beard and a character that embodied the heart of hospitality – a genuine desire to look after others and find joy in feeding people. He taught my mother how to make the most amazing curries at a fraction of the cost of other meals, and we kids loved the spices and aromas emanating from her kitchen. We could smell them before we even got to the front door.

Food has a funny way of making you feel safe and happy, lifting you up, even if just for a moment. The excitement among us kids on curry night was electric, especially if Mum had mastered a new recipe. It was our big family feast night and was like an exotic awakening. As a result, I love curries and feel strongly connected to them. For me, they're more than food – they are an embedded memory of joy during a tough period.

As an adult, that memory spurred a trip to Amritsar in northern India, the birthplace of butter chicken, because I wanted to understand how it was made perfectly. But in the UK, I'd never really found anywhere that captured the way those curries I'd had as a nine-year-old had made me feel. Until, of course, I went to Newcastle in northeast England in 2022.

I was up there filming *Future Food Stars* and had been told of a new Indian restaurant called Khai Khai, so I went to check it out. I got there at half past six, hoping to get in and out before the evening rush, but it was already heaving with customers and full of energy. Nonetheless, I managed to get a table overlooking a beach, and I also had a clear view of the open-plan kitchen, where three chefs were plying their trade.

I ordered a tandoori-grilled mackerel with a masala sauce. It arrived, plated simply, but looked stunning.

The aromas had me salivating before I even managed a bite. What happened next was like a reawakening. I took a mouthful and I was floored. It was one of the most extraordinary fish dishes I had ever eaten – in Newcastle of all places!

The masala sauce, using a fresh blend of garam masala, was better than any I'd tasted before, and the mackerel was perfectly cooked. It was completely mind-blowing. It transported me all the way back to those early family curry nights, when Mum put her heart into every part of the dishes she'd learned from the landlord. The food wasn't the same, of course, but the way it made me feel was extraordinary. It was high quality with a depth, harmony and balance that stopped me in my tracks.

I took a photo of the dish and sent it to chef patron Matt Abé at Restaurant Gordon Ramsay and to group executive development chef Jocky Petrie with the message: 'I'm in Newcastle, and I've just had one of the best mackerel dishes in my entire life.' This goes to show that excellent food is about how it makes you feel, whatever the location.

We are living in interesting times, when the focus on seasonality and sustainability is greater than ever. We are also having to cope with the fall-out from the Covid-19 pandemic, the consequent recession and the spiralling cost of living. Recent events have made us rethink our existence and perhaps cook more thoughtfully, more seriously, remembering that food brings people together.

Inspired by my mackerel masala experience, I asked the Michelin-starred Indian chef Alfred Prasad to work with my team and come up with six amazing curries – two fish, two meat, two vegetarian – for use in my restaurant group. The results were extraordinary. The sauces were utter perfection, and their green papaya slaw was something I'd never had before.

The mackerel dish is something I could see on the menu at Royal Hospital Road, but I'd never have said that 25 years ago. We were just too focused on French-style cooking at the time. Now, though, if Matt wanted to do a sea bass with a masala sauce, I can see it happening. He has already found inspiration from his travels in Asia, creating a spin on Thai green curry sauce to serve with barbecued lobster tail and black fig chutney. The influences in our kitchen are truly global now. Our team members come from all around the world and our inspirations are equally international.

Restaurant Gordon Ramsay was built on my vision for a new, lighter approach to modern British food, and that approach continues to evolve. If, 10 years ago, I had said that a young Australian chef would be running a three-Michelin-star restaurant in Europe, I would have been laughed at. But Matt Abé has achieved just that, and I love the southern hemisphere vibe he has brought to the kitchen. It goes to show that food evolution is a powerful and dynamic thing. It crosses borders, jumps language barriers, fills us with joy, sustains us, inspires us, helps us to understand each other and fills us with wonder.

Of course, you don't evolve by hiding behind the hotplate. Matt and I have gone on some extraordinary walkabouts, as I call them, crossing the world and immersing ourselves in the dining culture of different cities. He's moved on from the style that was Clare Smyth's legacy when she left Restaurant Gordon Ramsay, and that's as it should be. A great chef will evolve and keep moving forward.

On our travels, Matt and I become customers. We've rocked up to one-star and two-star restaurants, no-star tapas bars, been all through Scandinavia and immersed ourselves in San Francisco and Los Angeles. It's important to the future of Restaurant Gordon Ramsay to know what is going on across the planet, to discover what we love and what we don't.

We've allowed some of the ideas we came across to evolve into our modern British style, as you don't move forward by pigeon-holing yourself. We are a team, finding new ways and nuances that make Restaurant Gordon Ramsay better every single day. We are also guiding each member of our brigade to be their own chef, ready to take on the world and switch the lights on in their own restaurant one day. Everyone needs to have goals. You can't hold onto people and squeeze them too tightly because they'll pop. Giving them the foundation, the skills, the understanding to step out on their own is how we maintain the magic in our kitchen.

Part of nurturing our chefs is keeping them up to date with the world of food. When I hear of a restaurant that's creating a buzz, or there's a chance to eat at a hotspot, I'm on the telephone and then we're all piling onto a flight to experience it together. Often, they'll see something different from me, but still recognise what attracted me to that place to begin with. They come back from these trips with all sorts of nuggets that they want to incorporate, just as I did with Guy Savoy in Paris.

London is extraordinary, but it gets claustrophobic if you don't look beyond what it has to offer. I always say to my team, 'Big fish swim alone. Don't get caught in the school; learn to swim on your own.' It may be my name above the door, but the real talent, the heart of Restaurant Gordon Ramsay, is the team, both front and back of house. They are the people I can rely on to deliver the most special dining experience possible.

Of course, a lot happens in 25 years of someone's life, and in my case, it hasn't just been about the restaurant. Tana and I have built a family. We have five children who have all grown up as the restaurant has evolved and my career has branched off into all manner of extraordinary things around the world. Tana is the connective tissue, the glue that holds it all together in the background. She has shown such faith in me, and it is the love of her and the children that sustains me. They have also been very tolerant in allowing me to do what I do because they know I can't sit still. I must keep pushing forward, and I see that determination in all of them in different ways.

Tana has instilled lovely manners in the kids and they know how to conduct themselves at the restaurant. They always talk to the staff in a friendly and respectful way, and they never forget to go into the kitchen and thank the chef. I think this shows they are well grounded, taking nothing for granted, and I am so proud of them.

As for me, I think I've shown them what hard work can achieve, the necessity of having goals, and the importance of not resting on your laurels. My advice to them has been, 'You must do it because no one will do it for you. Aim high, and once you get there, aim higher.'

Although my kids have flirted with the idea of entering a career in hospitality, they've actually followed very different paths. Meg is working for the Metropolitan Police; Jack is in the military as a roaring commando; Holly is into fashion; Tilly is at university; and Oscar is a naughty four-year-old. This means I still haven't got a chef in the family who wants to take over, so I go to bed every night knowing that I have to continue, no matter what. It's good motivation!

Looking back over the last 25 years, I am proud of everything I've done, and Restaurant Gordon Ramsay is the pinnacle of what I've worked to achieve. Nonetheless, the staff and I continue to push every day, with eyes and ears wide open to possibilities, and paying the finest attention to detail.

The future for this extraordinary team and restaurant shines bright.

The Basics

These are recipes that we make and use so often in the kitchen that most of the chefs know them off by heart. They are the building blocks of many of our dishes, both sweet and savoury, and they rarely change. If something isn't broken, don't fix it. Here are our basic chicken, veal and vegetable stocks, our house vinaigrette and pickling liquor, the ratio for our stock syrup, the instructions for beurre noisette and saffron water, and the puff pastry recipe that never fails.

Chicken Stock

2kg chicken wings
1kg chicken necks
4 celery sticks, halved
2 onions, peeled and quartered
2 leeks, white parts only, quartered
6 garlic cloves, cracked with the blade
   of a chef's knife
10 thyme sprigs
1 bay leaf
10 white peppercorns

Put the chicken wings and necks into a large stockpot and cover with cold water. Bring to the boil over a medium heat, then discard the water. Cover with fresh cold water and add the remaining ingredients. Bring back to the boil, then reduce the heat to a gentle simmer for 4 hours, regularly skimming off any fat and impurities that rise to the surface. Pass through a fine-meshed sieve lined with muslin. Allow to cool over an ice bath, then keep in the fridge to be used as needed.

Veal Stock

4kg veal bones
100ml vegetable oil
4 carrots, peeled and roughly chopped
2 leeks, green parts only, roughly chopped
2 onions, peeled and roughly chopped
2 celery sticks
1 garlic bulb, halved
10 black peppercorns
10 thyme sprigs
100g tomato purée
1 bay leaf

Preheat the oven to 200°C no fan. Place the bones in a roasting tray with 50ml of the vegetable oil and roast in the oven for 60–90 minutes, turning every 20 minutes, until golden brown. Place a large stockpot over a medium heat and add the remaining oil. When hot, add the vegetables and cook until evenly caramelised. Next add the garlic, peppercorns, thyme and tomato purée and allow to cook for 1 minute before adding the roasted bones and generously covering with cold water. Bring to the boil, then reduce the heat to a gentle simmer and cook for 24 hours, regularly skimming off any fat and impurities that rise to the surface. If the level of the liquid goes below the bones, top up with more cold water. Pass through a fine-meshed sieve lined with muslin and transfer to a large, clean saucepan. Place over a medium heat and reduce the stock by half. Cool over an ice bath, then keep in the fridge to be used as needed.

Vegetable Nage

4 carrots, peeled and finely diced
1 leek, finely diced
2 onions, peeled and finely diced
4 celery sticks, finely diced
5 white peppercorns
5 black peppercorns
10 coriander seeds
2 star anise
1 bay leaf
300ml chardonnay wine
1 lemon, sliced
25g chervil and parsley stalks

Put all the vegetables into a wide saucepan and add the peppercorns, coriander seeds, star anise and bay leaf. Pour in just enough water to cover the vegetables, place over a high heat and bring to the boil. Add the wine and bring back to the boil. Remove the pan from the heat, add the lemon slices and herbs stalks and allow to infuse overnight. Strain through a fine-meshed sieve, then keep in the fridge to be used as needed.

Beurre Noisette

250g unsalted butter, diced

Put the butter into a medium saucepan over a medium–high heat and allow it to melt, caramelise and foam until it smells sweet and nutty. Remove from the heat and pass through a fine-meshed chinois lined with muslin. Allow to cool, then store in the fridge until required.

House Pickling Liquor

750ml chardonnay vinegar
750ml Stock Syrup (see overleaf)
20g fine sea salt

Put the vinegar and stock syrup into a saucepan with 1 litre water and bring to the boil over a medium heat. Remove from the heat and allow to cool. Use as required.

Vinaigrette

175ml champagne vinegar
500ml pomace oil
10g fine sea salt

Put all the ingredients into a bowl and mix together with a hand-held blender until emulsified. Check the seasoning and store until required.

Saffron Water

5g saffron strands

Put the saffron into a medium-sized saucepan with 750ml water, place over a medium heat and bring to the boil. Remove from the heat and allow to infuse for 5 minutes. Pass through a fine-meshed chinois, squeezing out all the water. Set aside to cool, then store in the fridge until required.

Stock Syrup

750g caster sugar
85g glucose

Put the sugar and glucose into a large saucepan with 675ml water and bring to the boil over a medium heat. Set aside to cool, then use as required.

Puff Pastry

Basic Dough
230g T45 flour, plus extra for dusting
60g cold unsalted butter, cut into
1cm cubes
8g fine salt

Butter Layer
210g soft unsalted butter, cut into
1cm cubes
70g T45 flour, plus extra for dusting

To make the basic dough, mix the flour, butter and salt to a crumb using your fingertips or a stand mixer – the texture should be sand-like. Add 145ml cold water and knead on a floured surface until the dough comes together. Form into a rectangle and score all over with a sharp knife to avoid shrinking. Wrap tightly in cling film and chill overnight.

For the butter layer, put the butter and flour into the bowl of a stand mixer and beat until it comes together. Form into a rectangle, wrap in baking paper and chill for 2 hours. Before making the pastry, let the butter layer soften at room temperature for 10 minutes.

Roll the dough into a large, narrow rectangle about 1cm thick – it should be three times as long as it is wide. Put the butter layer in the middle of the rectangle and fold the pastry over to make a book-shaped parcel, making sure the butter is sealed inside. Roll it out lengthways, keeping the same width, until it is three times as long as it is wide. Fold the edges into the middle of the rectangle, creating a second book-shaped parcel, then turn the pastry 90° and repeat the process. Keep the dough cold throughout by putting it in the fridge for 10 minutes every 15 minutes. Roll, fold and turn the pastry five times in all, making sure it stays cool. Wrap tightly in cling film and chill overnight. Use as required or freeze for later.

Conversion Chart

The cooking at Restaurant Gordon Ramsay requires precision, so we always work with metric measures. The equivalents to them given below are approximations and therefore the end results may be slightly different.

Oven temperatures

°C Fan	°C No fan	°F	Gas
90	110	225	¼
100	120	250	½
120	140	275	1
130	150	300	2
140	160	325	3
160	180	350	4
170	190	375	5
180	200	400	6
200	220	425	7
210	230	450	8
220	240	475	9

Dry measures

1.25g	¼ teaspoon
2.5g	½ teaspoon
5g	⅛oz / 1 level teaspoon
10g	¼oz
15g	½oz / 1 level tablespoon
20g	¾oz
25g	1oz
35g	1¼oz
40g	1½oz
50g	2oz
65g	2½oz
75g	3oz
90g	3½oz
100g	4oz (¼lb)
110g	4¼oz
120g	4½oz
135g	4¾oz
150g	5oz
165g	5½oz
175g	6oz
185g	6½oz
200g	7oz
215g	7½oz
225g	8oz (½lb)
250g	9oz
275g	10oz
300g	11oz
350g	12oz (¾lb)
375g	13oz
400g	14oz
425g	15oz
450g	16oz (1lb)
500g	18oz
550g	1¼lb
700g	1½lb
800g	1¾lb
900g	2lb
1kg	2¼lb
1.25kg	2½lb
1.5kg	3lb
2kg	4½lb
4kg	9lb
5kg	11lb
6kg	13lb
7kg	15lb

Liquid measures

250ml or 8fl oz = 1 US cup
500ml or 16fl oz = 1 US pint / 2 US cups

2.5ml	½ teaspoon
5ml	1 teaspoon
7.5ml	1½ teaspoons
10ml	2 teaspoons
15ml	1 tablespoon / ½fl oz
20ml	¾fl oz
25ml	1fl oz
35ml	1¼fl oz
40ml	1½fl oz
50ml	2fl oz
60ml	2¼fl oz
65ml	2½fl oz
85ml	3fl oz
100ml	3½fl oz
120ml	4fl oz
135ml	4½fl oz
150ml	5fl oz
175ml	6fl oz
200ml	7fl oz
250ml	8fl oz
275ml	9fl oz
300ml	10fl oz
325ml	11fl oz
350ml	12fl oz
375ml	13fl oz
400ml	14fl oz
450ml	15fl oz
475ml	16fl oz
500ml	17fl oz
550ml	18fl oz
575ml	19fl oz
600ml	20fl oz (1 UK pint)
750ml	26fl oz
900ml	31fl oz
1 litre	35fl oz
1.25 litres	44fl oz
1.5 litres	52fl oz
2 litres	70fl oz

Specialist Ingredients

As restaurant chefs working at the highest level, we rely on certain ingredients in the kitchen to bring flavour, structure and balance to our dishes, and these items aren't usually available in the supermarket. We have a fantastic range of suppliers who source unusual flavours from around the world so we can experiment with lesser-known ingredients, unexpected combinations and ambitious textures. Here is a guide to some of the ingredients that help us create perfection every day.

Agar agar

Agar agar is a plant-based gelatine derived from seaweed that is used to set gels and jellies. It has a higher melting point than regular gelatine, which means it stays reliably thick at room temperature and can be used warm without losing shape. It is perfect for our fluid gels and purées.

Black garlic

When regular garlic is aged using heat and humidity, it changes from white to darkest black. As the colour changes, so does the flavour, becoming more mellow over time, with sweet and sour notes of caramel, tamarind and molasses.

Calamansi

Also known as Philippine lime, calamansi is a citrus fruit that has the tartness of lemons and limes and the sweetness of oranges. We use the flesh of the fruit and calamansi vinegar to bring a unique flavourful sharpness to fish and shellfish dishes.

Citric acid

Citric acid is found naturally in citrus fruits – it's what makes them tart – but it is also manufactured for use as a preserving agent and flavour enhancer. We use it to add acidity without adding flavour or colour to sauces and purées.

Dashi vinegar

This is a Japanese vinegar that has been flavoured with the elements of dashi broth – kombu seaweed and katsuobushi dried tuna flakes – which impart an umami-rich mouthfeel and savoury flavour with a sweet sharpness not present in the original stock.

Dextrose powder

Dextrose is a simple sugar, like glucose, that is less sweet than sucrose (the sugar found in sugar cane and beets). We use it to dust the top of puff pastry during baking because it promotes browning and, when combined with icing sugar, creates the perfect shiny glaze.

Feuilletine

Feuilletine is made from very thin crêpes that have been allowed to become crisp and are then broken into tiny pieces. The crispy shards are used to add crunch to the bases of layered desserts, such as delices, or texture to ganaches, mousses or truffles.

Finger limes

Also known as citrus caviar, finger limes are pickle-shaped fruits native to Australia, which are full of beads of sweet and sour juice that burst in your mouth. They bring acidity and a unique texture to seafood dishes, desserts and cocktails.

Gellan F

Gellan F is a setting agent that has a higher melting point than both agar agar and gelatine; it can withstand temperatures up to 120°C, which means it can be used to give structure to hot purées, fluid gels and custards. It has the added advantage of being crystal clear and completely tasteless.

Hibiscus flowers

When dried, hibiscus flowers have a fruity tartness similar to cranberries, a wonderful deep red colour and an exotic fragrance that make them a popular ingredient for preserves, herbal teas and cocktails. We use them to flavour purées, mousses and cordials.

Katsuobushi flakes

Also known as bonito, katsuobushi flakes come from smoked, fermented and dried tuna, and are an essential ingredient in dashi, the foundation stock of Japanese cuisine. They are packed with umami and add a savoury smokiness to soups, noodle dishes and sauces.

Kombu

Like katsuobushi, kombu, a dried, edible seaweed, is a fundamental element of dashi. It is prized for its intense umami properties, which add a deep savouriness and mouthfeel to stocks, broths and sauces.

Makrut lime leaves

Historically known as kaffir lime leaves, makrut leaves are a key ingredient in Thai and Southeast Asian cooking. They are intensely aromatic, with the flavour and fragrance of citrus, but without those fruits' acidity.

Matcha powder

Matcha is very finely ground, high-quality green tea that is drunk all over Asia, but particularly in Japan, where it is at the heart of the traditional tea ceremony. It is most often used to flavour and colour puddings, cakes and sweets, but its slight bitterness and mild vegetal taste mean it can also be used in savoury dishes too.

Mignonette pepper

In the past, mignonette pepper referred to a French-Canadian spice mix made with black and white peppercorns and coriander seeds, but these days it is used to describe particularly coarsely ground pepper. We grind black pepper by hand, then sieve it several times to get consistently large pieces for seasoning and finishing dishes.

Nori

Nori is the dried seaweed that is used in sushi-making to wrap maki, nigiri and onigiri. Like all seaweeds, it is pleasantly salty and rich in umami, making it a great ingredient for boosting the savouriness of seafood and vegetarian dishes.

Oak-smoked water

This unusual ingredient allows us to recreate the wonderful flavour of smoked wood without having to find room for a smoker in the restaurant kitchen. Pure water is smoked over oak chips, turning it into a versatile condiment that we use to add depth and a sense of autumn and winter seasonality to our food.

Orgeat syrup

Made from almonds, sugar and orange flower water, orgeat syrup is a sweet cordial generally used in cocktails and non-alcoholic drinks. Its nutty almond flavour and distinct aroma add perfume, flavour and sweetness to creamy or baked desserts in a more subtle way than almond extract or amaretto would.

Pasteurised egg whites and yolks

As we often need egg whites without the yolks and vice versa, we use pasteurised egg whites and yolks that are supplied to the restaurant separately in liquid form. Not only does this cut down on wastage, it also means we can weigh them more precisely, leading to more consistent results.

Pectinex Ultra SP-L

Pectinex Ultra SP-L is a specialist ingredient used for breaking down pectin in fruit and fruit juices. We use it to effortlessly remove all the skin and pith from citrus fruits, leaving just the juicy segments behind.

Piment d'Espelette chilli powder

The chilli pepper grown in the Espelette region of southwest France is dried and ground to a powder. It has a mild heat and gentle smokiness that is a little like smoked paprika. A mainstay of Basque cuisine, it is our chilli powder of choice in the kitchen because it adds warmth and flavour without too much of a distracting hit of heat.

Procrema 100 Cold

Used as a stabiliser, Procrema 100 Cold gives ice cream the perfect creamy consistency while helping it to hold its shape at room temperature. We use it in all our ice creams to make sure our rochers and quenelles don't start to melt before they get to the table.

Sarawak pepper

This pepper, which comes from Borneo in the Sarawak state of Malaysia, is smaller and milder than regular black pepper, but what it lacks in heat, it makes up for in flavour and fragrance. It has a slight fruitiness and aromatic sweetness with a hint of citrus which make it an unexpected but delicious seasoning for fruit-based desserts.

Shio koji

A fermented rice condiment, shio koji is used to marinate and tenderise protein and, like so many Japanese ingredients, to add umami to a variety of dishes. It is made by fermenting rice that has been inoculated with the koji bacteria, which creates a loose, lumpy paste. Straining off the liquid creates a versatile ingredient for adding to stocks and sauces.

Sobacha

To make this Japanese buckwheat tea, the grains of buckwheat are roasted to caramelise the naturally occurring sugars, giving them a nutty, biscuity flavour and crisp texture. Rather than infusing them in water, we sprinkle them over salads and garnishes to add crunch.

Sodium citrate

The natural salt of citric acid, sodium citrate is used as a preservative and food additive. It has a particularly useful function in the restaurant kitchen because it prevents vulnerable cheese sauces from splitting, giving them a stable, smooth and creamy texture.

Soya lecithin

Soya lecithin is an emulsifier, stabiliser and preservative extracted from soya beans. We use it when making veloutés because it gives these velvety liquids structure, which helps to stabilise the bubbles when the sauce is aerated to create a foam.

Super neutrose

This special stabilising agent is used in sorbets and ice creams to prevent crystallisation as the base liquids freeze. It creates a smooth texture and a super-soft scoop that will hold its shape for longer at room temperature.

Trimoline

Trimoline is an inverted sugar, which means the sucrose molecules have been broken down into glucose and fructose, making it extra sweet. We use it in ice creams, ganaches and caramels because it prevents crystallisation.

Ultratex

This is a rapid-thickening starch that we use when making purées, gels and sauces. The powder can be used hot or cold, and is tasteless and colourless, so it doesn't affect the flavour while ensuring the smooth, creamy texture we are looking for.

Vegetable carbon

A natural food dye, vegetable carbon comes in the form of an odourless and flavourless powder. This means it can be added to sauces, ice creams and baked goods without affecting the taste, while creating an intense black colour that looks very dramatic on the plate.

Verjus

Made from the juice of unripe and unfermented grapes, verjus, or verjuice, is a mildly tart condiment that we use to bring an aromatic, sweet and gentle acidity to dishes that might be overwhelmed by harsher vinegar or lemon juice.

Vin jaune

Vin jaune, or yellow wine, comes from the Jura region of France, where it is made with the savagnin grape using a method similar to that used for sherry. Although it shares some characteristics with sherry, it isn't a fortified wine, so it doesn't have the same sweetness. It is very dry and very acidic, and is delicious to cook with.

Specialist Equipment

In the restaurant kitchen, much of what we do is done by hand, but we also rely on specialist catering equipment to make the labour-intensive jobs easier and to achieve a finish that is sometimes only possible with particular machinery. Here is a list of the heavy-duty and not-so-heavy-duty kitchen kit that we rely on every day to achieve the level of consistency and finesse expected from a three-Michelin-star restaurant.

Konro grill

A konro or hibachi grill is a small, portable brazier from Japan, where it is traditionally used for cooking yakitori over hot coals (binchotan) at the table. Because space is at a premium in the restaurant kitchen, the small size of the grill allows us to keep it for adding that inimitable charred, smoky flavour without taking up too much room.

Mandoline

Also known as a Japanese slicer, a madoline is a very sharp blade incorporated into a basic plastic frame that makes it easy to hold as vegetables are passed over it repeatedly to shave off very fine slices. Cutting vegetables in this way gives finer and more consistently sized slices than can be achieved by hand with a knife.

Micro scales

Cooking at a three-star level is all about consistency, and consistency is only really possible with precision. A dish needs to look and taste the same at every service, every day of the week, whoever is cooking it, so we follow precise recipes and use digital scales to measure ingredients rather than tossing in pinches and handfuls. Micro scales are able to register weights under 5g, making them very useful for weighing small amounts of powders, spices and salt.

Pacojet

A Pacojet machine micro-purées frozen ingredients to create the smoothest possible finish. We use it for making velvety purées and creamy sauces, but above all for churning ice cream. The custard base is frozen solid, then churned in the Pacojet just before service to give the lightest, smoothest ice cream imaginable.

Robot Coupe

This multi-function food processor is in constant use in the kitchen. Its industrial strength means it can chop any vegetable, raw or cooked, and effortlessly blitz hard ingredients, such as nuts and caramelised sugar, but it is also invaluable for blending, puréeing and kneading.

Siphon

A siphon, also known as an espuma gun, creamer or whipped cream dispenser, uses nitrous oxide (laughing gas) to inject tiny bubbles into liquids to create aerated sauces and foams. It can be charged with gas once for giving lightness to a velouté or sabayon, for example, or twice for a more bubbly foam.

Sous-vide machine and water bath

A sous-vide machine and a water bath are two pieces of equipment often used in conjunction with one another. Cooking 'sous-vide' is a technique that involves placing food in special bags that are then sealed under vacuum and placed in a temperature-controlled water bath, often for long periods of time. Cooking ingredients in this way has three great advantages over more traditional methods such as roasting or poaching. First, cooking meat, fish or vegetables in a sealed bag allows for maximum flavour retention, as no juices are lost during the process. Second, ingredients cook more evenly as they are surrounded by water rather than air, which is a much less efficient heat conductor. And third, setting the water bath to a fixed temperature allows absolute precision, so it is almost impossible to overcook things.

Sugar thermometer

When working with sugar, making jam or tempering chocolate, reaching precise temperatures is essential. Using a sugar thermometer takes any guesswork out of the process and produces the consistent and successful results we need in the pastry section every day.

Thermomix

A Thermomix is a very strong blender that can be heated to precise temperatures while blending, which means it is excellent for making infused oils, cooking custards and warming ingredients while blitzing. The heat function also allows us to activate setting agents, such as Gellan F, when making fluid gels or thickened purées.

Vegetable sheeter

A vegetable sheeter is a commercial-grade slicer for turning hard vegetables, such as beetroots, radishes and turnips, into very fine ribbons or sheets. It would be impossible to get the same ultra-fine results by hand, so we use a sheeter from Japan, where this is a standard piece of kitchen equipment for making garnishes.

Vitamix

A Vitamix is another high-powered blender in regular use in the restaurant kitchen. When heat isn't required, we use it instead of the Thermomix for blending gels, sauces and purées at speed, and blitzing dry ingredients to fine powders.

Index

Z

Acknowledgements

Gordon Ramsay

Every restaurant lives or dies on the strength of its team, but nowhere is this more true than in a three-Michelin-starred restaurant. I would like to take this opportunity to thank every member of staff, past and present, for making Restaurant Gordon Ramsay the success it has been for twenty-five years.

A huge thank you to my current chef patron Matt Abé, who has worked tirelessly to make this book as perfect as the food he serves every day. If they gave out stars for hard work, discipline and dedication alone, he would definitely deserve three! I'm immensely proud of you and the chef you are today.

The contribution of maitre d' Jean-Claude Breton to the success of Restaurant Gordon Ramsay cannot be overstated. Your passion, insight and dedication are like no other's, and have been the heart and soul of our restaurant for 25 years. JC, my friend, you are simply the best!

As always, thank you to my family. To Tana, without whose confidence, trust and patience RGR would never have existed – thank you for believing in me. And thanks, of course, to my grown-up children Megan, Holly, Jack and Tilly, and the not-so-grown-up Oscar. Don't tell Michelin, but you are the five stars that matter most to me.

I am grateful every day for my team who work so hard to make my busy life easier: Rachel Ferguson, Laura Giarrusso and Justin Mandel for ensuring every hour of every day counts, and finding me eight days in a week; Andy Wenlock and Lisa Edwards for leading my businesses with the heart and integrity I built them on; James 'Jocky' Petrie for your dedication and culinary genius; and Jo Milloy for your straight talking and unwavering support as my trusted publicist. I couldn't do it without you all.

I have also been very lucky to have had a great editorial team on my side for this project. Thank you to Anthony 'Huck' Huckstep for travelling to the other side of the world to immerse yourself in mine, and writing the words that tell my story, my way. It's always a pleasure to spend time in your company. To Camilla Stoddart for your skill and enthusiasm, and to the ever-patient Trish Burgess for keeping them both in check!

And then there's the talented people who have created this beautiful book, namely photographer John Carey, designer Al Rodger and production supremo Claudette Morris. Thank you all so much.

And finally, for giving me the chance to celebrate the success of Restaurant Gordon Ramsay in this special book, I have to thank Nicky Ross and her brilliant team at Hodder & Stoughton. In particular, thank you to Olivia Nightingall, Vickie Boff and Alainna Hadjigeorgiou for doing what they do so well.

Matt Abé

First and foremost, I would like to thank Gordon for his support and the belief he has shown in me, not least by giving me this opportunity to share our passion and dedication to our craft.

Big thanks to Kim Ratcharoen, Eduardo Polverino and Jack Alastair: nothing I do in the restaurant would be possible without their assistance and everyday support. I would also like to thank my incredible team, both back and front of house, for their constant commitment and dedication.

Thanks also to editor Camilla Stoddart for her help with the words, and to photographer John Carey, whose pictures bring our vision to life.

Finally, for always believing in me, I would like to thank my parents, Ray and Leonie Abé.

'One team one dream.'

First published in Great Britain in 2023 by Hodder & Stoughton
An Hachette UK company

1

A CIP catalogue record for this title is available from the British Library

Hardback ISBN 978 1 473 65231 6
eBook ISBN 978 1 473 65233 0

Contributing Editor: Anthony Huckstep
Editorial Director: Nicky Ross
Project Editor: Olivia Nightingall
Project Manager and Copy Editor: Patricia Burgess
Design and Art Direction: Praline (Al Rodger and David Tanguy)
Photography: John Carey
In-house Art Direction: Alasdair Oliver
Production Manager: Claudette Morris

Colour origination by Alta Image London
Printed and bound in China by C&C Offset Printing Co., Ltd.

Hodder & Stoughton policy is to use papers that are natural,
renewable and recyclable products and made from wood grown
in sustainable forests. The logging and manufacturing processes
are expected to conform to the environmental regulations of the
country of origin.

Hodder & Stoughton Ltd
Carmelite House
50 Victoria Embankment
London
EC4Y 0DZ

www.hodder.co.uk